Boy *from the* Moor

His Life, Adventures and
Sudden Disappearance

To Dave,

Best wishes and

happy reading

Boy *from the* Moor

His Life, Adventures and Sudden Disappearance

Helen Balkwill

Elsie E E Publishing

A catalogue record for this title is available from the British Library.

ISBN: 978–1–916137–60–8

Printed by Platinum Press of Dunstable
Designed by Sophie Honeybelle and Peter Hawkes
at Hawkes Design & Publishing Ltd

Elsie E E Publishing
elsiepublish@gmail.com

'Je est un autre...'

Arthur Rimbaud, *Lettre du Voyant*

CONTENTS

Preface and Acknowledgements

I have spent almost a lifetime wanting to tell this story. It began in 1969 when, as a child of only eight, I was told that my father had died in an unexplained traffic accident in Aden. I wanted to scream out to the world that I could not believe it. But inexplicably I was prevented from doing so by some of the adults who surrounded me. Crazy experiences I had had with my dad in Aden and around the world supported my incredulity, but I was not allowed to talk about those early days of my childhood. However, I was not to be eternally silenced and, as an adult, launched an investigation into the unexplained mystery of my dad's death. It has been twenty-five years since I started this journey and after an exhaustive search, I have come to the conclusion that it's time to present my findings. The story is not complete and I am sure that there are facts, events and people just waiting to be discovered that might fill in the gaps.

I would like to begin the credits here by honouring my parents, Peter the eponymous *Boy from the Moor* and Joan Balkwill, without whom there would be no story, no adventure, no mystery. Those two knew how to live and they took my brother and me along on their thrilling ride for as long as it lasted. Also my children, Cecilia and Peter, who are my beloved family now.

The people from many walks of life who assisted me in my twenty-five years of searching to find out what happened to my father are too numerous to mention individually in person and, because my investigation started so long ago, many have now sadly passed away. Both in Aden and London, a number of Yemenis have helped me immeasurably but would prefer not to have their names included here. However, I could not miss this opportunity formally to thank the following: Tricia Glazer who has been a constant source of practical and emotional support from almost the beginning of my quest. Ernie and Kim Whitmarsh, Alan and Sue Offer, Ted Weinel, Ray Shoebridge, Trevor and Sandra Ellis, Jack Kennedy, Norah Neville, John and Marianne Warren, Alan Darling, Margaret Cole, Don Cudmore, Olive Balkwill, Stuart Balkwill, Kath Westcott, Derek Saunders and Liz Webber all took time to share their memories of my father with me. Ivor Lucas and Noel Brehony kindly assisted with guidance concerning Foreign Office protocol of the time, in particular about the Embassy in Aden. Not forgetting the Royal British Legion and Alan Wyle, with whom I travelled to Aden and who supported and comforted me when I was unable to find my father's grave there.

I would also like to thank Amy Ooi who set up the *Boy from the Moor* blog site, showed me how to use it and then sent me on my way with the story I so wanted to tell. The British Yemeni Society, in particular BYS members Adel Aulaqi and Thanos Petouris, encouraged me unfailingly in this project. Advice and information have generously been contributed by Keith McCloskey and Ron Smith (about aviation), Maria Holt (Middle Eastern affairs) and Jonathan Wilkins, Jennifer Drummond-Harris and Sheila Pratt (about life in colonial Aden). Pamela and Terry were kind enough to let me include a chapter about their experience of the chaotic days of newly independent Aden. Ted Weinel helped enormously in writing pieces for the Sudan chapters. Jack Clark supported my research about British national service in Egypt by describing his time as a young army serviceman there.

Finally I am grateful to those who have guided and supported this rookie author through the publishing process of this book: Peter Hawkes and Sophie Honeybelle at Hawkes Design and Publishing Limited, Hannah Aulaqi, Stephen Siu, Rosa Owen-Smith for her patient proof reading and Safa Mubgar and Ana Capone for their general publishing and PR advice.

The amount of advice and goodwill I have received for my investigation, and then my writing and publishing of *Boy from the Moor*, first as a blog and then as this book, has been staggering as well as a source of great personal gratification. However, in acknowledging this help, I would like to make clear that any inaccuracies and judgements offered within the book are my own responsibility.

Foreword

I am honoured that Helen has asked me to write the foreword for her remarkable and moving book about the father she lost when she was only eight years old. I never met Peter Balkwill, as he died a few weeks before I took up a post at the British Embassy in Aden at the end of January 1970. However, I feel I have met him now after reading how Helen brings Peter to life through talking to those who encountered him during his lifetime.

I first met Helen in 2011 when she contacted me to ask if I could throw any light on the circumstances of his death. She had read my book about the PDRY (Yemen Divided) and noticed that I was in Aden at around the same time. Unfortunately, I could not offer much help. I recalled that I had been aware of his death, but not of the details or of the assistance his family and his employer Airwork had been given by the embassy. During my time in Aden, several Airwork personnel were still present and working as normal with the South Yemeni Air Force. The British community in Aden itself was tiny, although there were still quite a few personnel working with BP in Little Aden where they continued to frequent the Bureika Club mentioned by Helen in this book.

The country (then the People's Republic of South Yemen) had been independent for just over two difficult years. The National Liberation Front (NLF) had only started to negotiate with the British nine days before its chaotic takeover on 30th November, 1967. Divisions within the organisation that had been put aside during the independence campaign disrupted and destabilised government until June 1969. At this point, the extreme left took over and set about creating a Marxist regime, changing the name of the country in the process. All this was happening in the period after Helen arrived in Aden as a small girl. She talks of her mother's memory of the tensions that were present, as well as the readiness of Airwork's staff to leave the country at very short notice. As she says, *"unless one personally experiences it, it is hard to truly know what it is like living the legacy of seismic global events, and how it affects ordinary people's everyday existence."* All this is vividly described from the point of view of the young girl in Chapter Eleven.

Aden's economy had been devastated by the closure of the Suez Canal in 1967 (it did not re-open until 1975), the loss of subsidies and jobs associated with the British presence, a mass exodus of those that were concerned about their possible fate under the new regime and attacks across the country's borders by the regime's many opponents. In early 1970 I found that, despite the pervasive atmosphere of fear, the remaining British were left alone and the government was not unfriendly to us personally. Having said that, they constantly attacked our past and present policies. It was unlike the chaos and upheaval of the 1967–69 period that Helen's family had to live through. We could be affected by government policy in odd ways. I arrived at Gold Mohur (mentioned by Helen), which was still one of the main meeting points for British and other nationals, to find that the small sailing boat I had inherited from a departing British diplomat had been 'nationalised' that morning along with the club and was now a 'people's boat'. However, I was granted exclusive use for the rest my stay, as were my successors. On the other hand, the Indian owners of Bhicagee Cowasjee (which Helen also mentions) faced a very difficult period. I was recently contacted by the daughter of one of the brothers running the company who was trying to write her family history. Yemenis working for the embassy were at risk: one who disappeared in 1972 was later found murdered.

Helen has searched everywhere and talked to everyone she could find that knew — or knew of — her father. She takes us through that journey, starting with the letter that devastated her family. The stories told by those she encountered paint vivid pictures of Peter as a much-loved boy surrounded by his aunts, a shy but dependable National Serviceman, as well as his long courtship of Helen's mother Joan while he was leading a peripatetic life supporting crop-spraying aircraft. She writes of the pain caused by the disappointments of not being able to find his final resting place.

The photos of Aden in Chapters Three and Four will bring back memories to all those who lived in Aden during the 1960s and 70s. Some of the buildings remained, albeit changed and damaged, when I last visited in the 2010s. The city itself has grown enormously outside the central areas shown in the photos. Much of the fighting in the early stages of the current war in mid-2015 was in these central areas and reports of the damage done are disturbing.

All who read this book will benefit from Helen's intrepid and determined research over a long period of time, as well as her ability to write in such an engrossing and vivid style. There is much that is fascinating in this book: the life stories of Peter's friends and relatives; the insights into life in Aden in its last days as a British colony and the first of those in the new republic. But what comes out most strongly is the respect and love of Peter, his zest for life and the impact on the life of a girl of eight years old losing her much-loved father. It is informative, interesting and poignant.

Dr Noel Brehony, CMG, former Chairman of The British-Yemeni Society and author of *Yemen Divided, The Story of a Failed State in South Arabia.*

Boy from the Moor

Chapter One

The Letter

View towards Dartmoor from Hatherleigh Moor.
Hatherleigh: As I Saw It, Eileen Gold

Peter Balkwill, circa 1968.

Peter John Balkwill, who was born in Hatherleigh, Devon, UK on 19th June 1926, died in Aden, South Yemen on 21st December 1969. Peter was my father, and at the time of writing I am approaching the 50th anniversary of his death. Throughout those 50 years I have come to discover that the circumstances of his passing, as well as of his time working in Aden, were mysterious to say the least. I have spent several of those years either wondering about or investigating the mystery of his death.

Peter is the eponymous Boy from the Moor and this is both the story of his life and untimely death, as well as an account of my search for the truth about him.

Hatherleigh, 1989

'They thought he was dead when he was born, they did.'

The old woman stirred in her corner armchair and turned towards the front parlour's only window.

'But somehow he survived ... the poor little mite.'

A small tug, with claw-like fingers, on a dingy net curtain brightened the room. Sunlight danced on time-warped furnishings, momentarily irradiating the fusty atmosphere with its sparkles, before bowing out as suddenly as it had arrived and then the curtain then fell from her grasp.

I could not tell whether her reluctance to hold the net curtain open was because of the weakness of her arthritis-wracked hand, or because, at her great age and with a weary look on her face, the outside world was no longer a place she wished to face.

'She gave birth one more time she did ... another boy ... but that one definitely didn't come oorrff.'

Speaking in a Devon accent as rich as local West Country clotted cream, the old lady was my great aunt Olive. The woman she spoke of was her sister-in-law — my grandmother, Margaret. Margaret's baby that had so miraculously survived at birth was to become in later years my father, Peter Balkwill, her only child.

I was in the Balkwill hometown of Hatherleigh, on undulating Hatherleigh Moor, which lies between the expanse of Dartmoor to the south and the rugged north Devon coast. The county city of Exeter is some 30 miles to the southeast. With the changing of the seasons, this countryside is a rolling patchwork of colourful, textured moorland vegetation, as well as a stark, ever-reaching wintry landscape, challenged by the strongest elements. It is beautiful mutable scenery in all its forms.

My great aunt and I were sitting in the house that her father and his brother had clubbed together to buy for her family when she was a girl. Unmarried her entire life, she had lived continuously at 10 Park Road ever since.

Despite her advancing age, Olive had still bothered to open up the front parlour specially to entertain me. This struck me as awe-inspiringly poignant, as it was as many as 15 years or more since she had done so for my childhood visits to the house.

1   2

In keeping with generations-old tradition, the property's formal room had always been kept closed and preserved for special occasions only. The best and most expensive furniture and fittings had barely been touched down the years, much less enjoyed by the family that had lived, breathed, played, laughed, loved and grieved together in this home. I looked around and imagined all of the characters now. Some of them I had never known. Some I had met in their older age when I was still too young to really know or understand them. Overwhelmingly though, I was touched by personal memories.

As a child, I had sat in this very room on at least one occasion every year with my own nuclear family on duty visits to the Devon Balkwills. These visits always comprised an attractively presented afternoon tea of home prepared local food such as ham, pickles, bread, cake and scones and cream. As far as my memory served me, nothing at all around me had changed: solid, dark furniture that I recognised, familiar velour drapes, a remarkable clock and pictures on the wall. Even the smell in the air was just the same.

I had travelled especially from London to interview Aunt Olive. The year was 1989 and she was 90 years old. I was 27 at the time.

My father had been tragically killed when I was a child. Margaret, along with my grandfather, Sam, who was Olive's older brother, and all of my many paternal relatives that I had known on the childhood summer holiday visits, were now dead.

Having grown up abroad and away from my father's roots, there were scenarios, personalities, and supposed scandals within his family that I wished to explore, now that I had reached adulthood and had begun to look back. I hoped that, as the last survivor, Olive would be able to answer my questions and shed light on my imaginings, before all would be lost.

I hoped particularly that Olive would talk to me about my father, Peter. Hoped she would share with me memories of the nephew that she had known as a boy, and tell me what she knew about him as a young man once he had left Hatherleigh; how he had trained as an aircraft fitter, carried out his national service, moved around, met and married my mother during his travels, lived abroad and started his family. Hoped she would build a picture for me, and help me to understand the father that I had lost at only eight years old, and who I had, really, barely ever known. She had begun by telling me the story of his survival at birth, but I yearned to know more. Much, much more.

Most of all I hoped that Great Aunt Olive might be able to shed family light on the unfathomable mystery that had long surrounded the untimely, and supposedly accidental, death of my father in the Middle East.

The death of my father had been a mystery that had been confounding me and breaking my heart by turns for the last 18 years.

1. Olive and I in the garden of the Park Road house, circa 1968.

2. A young Olive (far left) as bridesmaid for her sister, Daisy in 1932.

Cambridge, 1969

The letter about my father's death was sent from his place of work in South Yemen the day after representatives from the British company, Airwork Services Limited, had arrived at our house in Cambridge, UK to inform my mother of the death in person. My father had reportedly been killed the day before that.

I did not have sight of the letter until 1988, almost 20 years after my father's death. It is the reading of the letter that triggered my 1989 visit to Aunt Olive. My mother had dug it out in order to answer questions that I had been increasingly pressing on her. Historically, Mum had refused to discuss my dad's death, and, indeed, anything to do with his and our time in Aden. Even when I was small she had sought to silence me on the subject. 'Death', she had always told me, 'is not a subject to be talked about.' She had conveniently revived the Victorian protocol she had learned whilst growing up from her parents and grandparents to establish a cover up. I had always felt it.

I had seen enough intrigue for myself during the few short years of my childhood in which my father had been alive to instinctively know that my mother was flannelling me. Our family life in the Middle East had always been "colourful". As I was growing into adulthood, however, I was becoming increasingly less inclined to accept the whitewash, and more and more determined to strike out for answers.

For the 25 years that had passed between my father's death abroad and the time that I had begun my investigations, I had had only my own personal memories from the time as reference to what had happened to my dad. Now I needed to establish facts, and this letter was to be only the beginning of a long, involved search.

Meanwhile, the black, cold December evening on which the men in dark coats from the Airwork headquarters in Bournemouth had come into our home became etched on my mind forever.

The sight of my mother is unforgettable. She was in an armchair, shaking violently whilst absent-mindedly stroking at the family dog who sat, head cocked questioningly, at her feet as Christmas baubles twinkled under electric light behind her.

I was eight years old.

HEADQUARTERS,
SOUTH YEMEN AIR FORCE,
KHORMAKSAR,
ADEN,
PEOPLE'S REPUBLIC OF SOUTHERN YEMEN.

23rd December 1969

Mrs. Joan Irene Balkwill,
8 Sefton Close,
Trumpington,
Cambridge.

Dear

It is with deep regret that I have to write to you today, and give you the sad details of your husband's death.

He was hit by a vehicle travelling at high speed at about 7 P.M. on Sunday 21st December 1969, at Maalla near the Cold Storage Building. The vehicle did not stop and the police are searching for it. Peter was rushed to hospital, but was dead on arrival, with a skull fracture.

I realise that nothing I say can relieve your terrible loss, but I hope you will get at least some small comfort from the many sincere messages of condolence I have received here on your behalf. Peter Balkwill was well known and well liked by everybody.

The burial service was this morning at Maalla cemetary, conducted by the Revd. Ian Findlay who is writing to you separately. There was a very large congregation, all the European population was well represented and there were many local people present.

Under separate cover I will be sending you photographs and a tape recording of the ceremony, and regretfully, copies of the death certificate.

Separate arrangements are being made for Peter's effects to be sent home, and you may safely leave all those things to me. If there is any other way I can help, please write and I will do all I can.

Yours very sincerely,

(G. Tombling)

Boy from the Moor

Chapter Two

Boy From The Moor

In Hatherleigh, circa 1936.

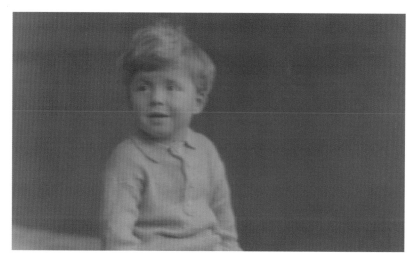

The Balkwills were fond of recording their lives in studio portraits. This one of Peter is from circa 1928.

The Balkwills

According to *Balkwill Genealogy Extracts*, a book published in 1908 by one Alfred Payne Balkwill, a copy of which is kept at Exeter Public Library in Devon, the Balkwill story begins in the early 1300s. A Plantagenet knight by the name of Robert de Bacquielle (pronounced Bagwil) was granted lands in Cheshire. Robert's surname is the common root from which the modern surnames of Baldwin, Bakewell, Baskerville and Balkwill are all derived.

Probably due to the need for good farmland, some of Robert's descendants migrated south to Devon. The first recorded entry of a Balkwill in the parish registers of Devon, at a time when registers first began, is the marriage of Francis Balkwill to Sarah in 1585 at Newton Abbot in the south of the county. It is very likely though that the Balkwills were established in Devon long before that date.

A branch of the Balkwill family has thrived in south Devon until this day. Other family members migrated to the moors of north Devon, and it is through two separate strains of these Balkwills that my father, Peter Balkwill, is descended. In fact, it is true to say that his paternal grandmother, Sarah Ann (born 1870), was so closely related to both strains that not only was her married surname Balkwill, but also her maiden name!

I find it interesting to note that my family name of Balkwill is so closely related to that of Baskerville, given the geography involved. Although

Hatherleigh, when travelling by road, seems some considerable distance from Dartmoor, the two actually lie only six and a half miles apart from each other. From Hatherleigh Moor excellent views of Dartmoor can be seen. Most Devonians regard Dartmoor as the heart of their county and are in awe of its rugged beauty, timelessness and the mystery that surrounds it. Over 100 years ago, Arthur Conan Doyle set what has become arguably one of the most famous thriller detective novels ever written on Dartmoor: The Hound of the Baskervilles.

Almost certainly Conan Doyle's fictional Baskerville family has roots in a reality that was closely related to Peter's forebears, and the atmospheric setting for the tale is actually the region that he and his family came from.

It seems fitting that such a life-long maverick character as Peter Balkwill, who ultimately died in mysterious circumstances in a land far flung from home, should have sprung from such notorious roots.

Hatherleigh 1926

Of the few things that are certain about my father's life, the following is for sure. Peter John Balkwill was born on 19th June 1926 in Hatherleigh to Samuel James Balkwill and Margaret Helen Balkwill, née Bulleid. He was the couple's first and only surviving child.

The exact location of the birth, however, is unclear. Sam and Margaret were living with a wealthy gentleman in his comfortable home in the town centre. Olive had told me, during my 1989 interview with her, that 'Old Man Ellacott', as he came to be known, had made an arrangement with the couple that they would care for him in his dotage in return for the accommodation. This was a concept that she and I discussed for some time as I

Old Man Ellacott.

struggled to comprehend a time before social care and the National Health Service. It is likely that Peter was born in Old Man Ellacott's home.

Sam and Margaret were struggling financially at the time. Sam had been a private in the trenches of World War I. He had returned to Hatherleigh, and to Margaret, having been gassed by the enemy during the conflict. The gassing of Sam was eternally blamed by the family for his inability to sustain employment or make an energetic contribution to family life with Margaret.

"Mustard gas, it was". I heard it said so many times when visiting the Devon relatives in the past. Even my mother was given to referring to the gassing of Grampy during my childhood, when exasperated at the running around required of her as my grandma grew older and less capable of caring for her infirm husband.

Years later I was able to establish for myself pretty much what had happened to Grampy in World War I. This came from information gleaned from his war medals, which had been left to me on the death of Grandma Margaret in 1988.

In 2005, research at The National Archives at Kew revealed that Grampy's two medals were the British War Medal and the Allied Victory Medal. His medal card was found, and this showed that he had been 38069 Private Samuel J Balkwill, Royal Berkshire Regiment. His battalion is not listed. Indeed, Sam's records could not be found. Apparently, all had been filmed but about 60% had been destroyed in the subsequent Blitz, the World War II offensive of 1940/41, which concentrated on the systematic bombing of industrial targets and civilian centres in London. Either his filmed records perished in that carnage or have been misfiled.

I also discovered that, because he did not have the 1914 or 1914–15 Star, Sam did not enter an operational theatre until after 31st December 1915. This, plus further research into chemical weapons used during World War I, has helped me to narrow down the type of gas that Sam would have been subjected to, the effect, physical and emotional, that this would have had on him, and the legacy it would have left.

So mustard gas, which was introduced by Germany in 1917, likely was the chemical agent that had permanently disabled Sam, changing his health and the way he would live his life forever, just as I had always heard.

Delivered in artillery shells, mustard gas was heavier than air and would settle to the ground in an oily liquid. It is not a particularly lethal agent but it would have polluted the battlefield and disabled the enemy, in this case my grandfather. The victim would suffer blistered skin, sore eyes, internal as well as external bleeding, and stripping of the mucous membrane in the bronchial tubes.

I remember Grampy, well into his 80s, sat in his fireside chair in the house in Exeter that was his and Margaret's final home, suffering choking spasms and fighting for breath. He hardly had energy to walk. He had survived the war and the mustard gas, but not the legacy of either.

Sam and Margaret enjoying a final picnic together by the River Tor before he left for World War I.

So, owing to Sam's disability, Margaret was left with responsibility for the family. She took a job in a bank and another in a school office to make ends meet. I think this is why my dad quickly became a self-sufficient child.

The Balkwills were unusual in Hatherleigh come the end of World War I. They enjoyed the happy distinction that both of the family's sons, Sam and his older brother John, survived. Sam also had three sisters slightly younger than himself; Elsie, Amy and Olive, and a baby sister called Daisy.

Park Road, where the family lived, leads to a small town square which is bordered by a pub, a coaching inn and, on its north side, a church yard which follows a hillock up towards the town's 15th century church, St John the Baptist. On my 1989 family history visit to Olive, I took a stroll from Park Road towards the church, intending to catch a view of the rolling moorland from its vantage point. Entering by the churchyard lychgate from the square, I quickly came across the town's war memorial. A sad sight of a wheel cross sitting atop a fat granite plinth, weighted with the names of the town's World War I dead, etched in black. And there I quickly understood the great sadness of Elsie, Amy and Olive and the generation of Hatherleigh women who lost the menfolk who could and would have been their boyfriends, lovers, husbands.

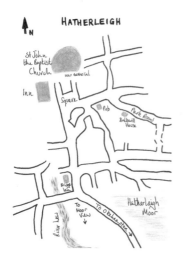

Thus, my father Peter, an only child after the death of his baby brother at birth, was surrounded in childhood by, from both sides of his family, no fewer than five maiden aunts whose main occupation became instructing, observing and generally interfering with the only child of Peter's generation in the family. These aunts gave my dad yet one more reason to break out for the peace and freedom of the surrounding moorland. The bitterness that they felt at having lost their men and their futures on the battlefields of Europe was also a burden the carefree boy had to bear right through into adulthood and marriage with my mother.

This is not to say that Peter was not adored and made to feel secure by his extended family of adult members. Not according to a childhood friend of his by the name of John Warren, who contacted me from his home in south Devon in the late 1990s to talk about my dad. By all accounts the well-meaning aunts, one uncle and the Balkwill grandparents at Park Road, Sarah and Samuel, were oblivious to the frustration they caused the precious child with their interfering ways. Peter learned early to walk the fine line between respecting his elders and pursuing his own agenda of self-fulfilment.

According to John, Peter grew into a very well-liked boy who went on to attend grammar school in nearby Okehampton with him. They later did national service together in Egypt, where Peter and other Hatherleigh lads befriended yet more young men from all around the UK, having been thrown together in a foreign and dusty land. John was in no doubt that Peter's amiable disposition and ability to socialise and network within friendship groups was down to the early life lesson he had learned in having to get on with his relatives.

Hearing this about the dad I lost so long ago was comforting. From the short time I had with him, I remember clearly being the little girl at his side as he would go about cultivating contacts and maintaining friendships and relationships. It would be visiting someone's house here, dropping in on a bar there, and even, occasionally, being taken to his workplace at the airport. It was good to learn how close to, what I now learned was, the real essence of my father I had actually been.

And as I watch my children grow to adulthood, it is awe-inspiring to see them manifesting versions of these traits of the grandfather they never knew. It is a privilege to know that this will have been the result of me passing to the new generation such a positive legacy that will surely serve them well in life, borne out of my dad's difficult formative experience almost a century ago.

So, conversations with Olive and with John helped me to piece together a jigsaw picture of my dad's childhood, how this moulded him, and the legacy he has left behind.

Beginning life at Old Man Ellacott's in the heart of the town, a stone's throw from the Balkwill house at Park Road and all local amenities, Peter would, from a young age, take himself from one haunt to another. To his school, for example, to the shops, dropping in on his mother at work, on up to the Balkwill house for, as Olive fondly remembered, freshly baked after school treats. And invariably on out to the nearest reaches of the moor, before arriving exhausted for bed back at the family lodgings with the old man. Learning this about his early years helped me to understand, once and for all, the itinerant and adventurous lifestyle my dad was to go on to live.

In mid childhood, yet one more tragedy was to befall Peter's parents that was to change the course of his young life. Old Man Ellacott died.

The death of the old man had not, of course, been entirely unexpected. But the disappointment, particularly for Margaret, as Olive reported it to me, was that Old Man Ellacott did not leave the house or any bequests to the young family, as had been hoped that he might. Not just hoped, but relied upon. It might strike us as unusual, but accounts I have heard suggest that this was the way that the small-town kind of society was back in those days of post-Victorian and inter-war hardship. John Warren urged me to consider that, rather than acting out of greedy expectation, my grandmother had been motivated by self preservation and caring for her family when banking on inheriting from her patron.

So it was that Sam, Margaret and the young Peter found themselves homeless. A headache for the ever-resourceful Margaret, who eventually found a cure with a move to the edge of town into a modern council house in Moor View. In those days, the house had a view of the rolling hills of Dartmoor, but in modern times this has been obscured by development.

I have visited the Moor View house. John Warren introduced me to its current inhabitant, Don Cudmore, who now privately owns the property and was kind enough to show me around. It is a bright, comfortable semi-detached house with good size gardens to the front and back. It sits in the middle of a single row of identical houses.

Not a bad move for the needy little family. But, according to Olive, a bit of a come down for Margaret. By no means a snob, it is nonetheless hard to imagine in this day and age the stigma that Margaret would have felt at leaving a large comfortable property for social housing. So much emotion in those days was wrapped up in an archaic class system and local gossip.

But Margaret, Sam and Peter got on with it and, according to John Warren, came to settle there reasonably happily until sometime after Peter left home. Indeed, my mother remembered her first visit to the in-laws was at Moor View.

John Warren recounted some of the pursuits his friend, Peter, came to enjoy whilst living at Moor View. He told me that Peter would spend time with his father fishing in the River Lew, which rushes and burbles over polished pebbles, in just the way that so many spectacular Devonshire rivers do, out from the town by Moor View. And as the boy came of age, I recall John telling me, the father would take the son to the Bridge Inn on the edge of town for a very quick drink before returning to Margaret at the house. John remembered visiting the family at Moor View, and other friends of Peter's collecting there. It was a small, but sociable and inclusive family.

In a 2006 visit I made to Hatherleigh, Don Cudmore took me to visit long term local octogenarian resident Kathleen Westcott. The enthusiastic reception I got from Kath was humbling. When she died in 1992, Great Aunt Olive had been the last of the Balkwills in Hatherleigh. Kath was excited to meet a descendant of a family that she had once known well, grown up with and been friends with. I felt, in the warmth of her embrace, that I was living the legacy of her good-hearted friendship with my forebears. She stepped back and surveyed my appearance. I carried the round hazel eyes and wavy hair both of my father and also of my grandmother, she informed me confidently.

With my true Balkwill credentials established, Kath sat me down in a cosy living room with traditional turn of the last century picture windows that looked out towards the moor. It was summertime and the view was glorious.

She explained to me her connection with the Balkwills. It seems that she had been close to a local family by the name of Manaton. One of the Manatons had been married to Sam's older brother John. They were a pleasant and humorous couple that was childless. They doted on my father, Kath said, little knowing that she was confirming to me yet again the strong Balkwill family ownership of my dad in his boyhood. Kath also told me that her younger brother had known Peter, with whom he had attended grammar school. She told me that he described my dad, just as John Warren had done, as being a sociable lad, with a particular gang of friends: Les Tellam and Des Hooper. She put names and gave life to characters appearing in the anecdotes about my father that had been told to me over the years. Peter, Kath told me, with a fond glint in her eye, was also a prankster.

Although disinclined to talk about my father after his passing in 1969, it had been my mother that had spoken to me from time to time about what she knew of his childhood. She talked of the same issues, which she had heard about from my father, but they came with a different slant from her than how I heard of them from the Devon folks.

For instance, my mother's understanding of the jokes and tricks that my father played during his teens, particularly, apparently, on the school bus from Hatherleigh to Okehampton, was that he was looking to, and did indeed, get himself expelled. He wanted out of school and on with adult life, she told me. However, Kath insisted that her brother had reported that it was all good fun, and Peter the more popular for it. He was, she said, never expelled.

Another issue of contention was the Temperance movement. Everyone — Mum, Olive, John Warren, Kath Westcott — all agreed that my father had been enrolled by the Balkwill family in the Hatherleigh branch of the Temperance movement as a child. Where Mum and the folks in Devon differed is whether my dad enjoyed the experience or not.

The Temperance movement was a social movement, which began around the 1820s. With a strong focus on the working class and children, members sought to influence as many people as possible to "sign the pledge" to abstain from alcohol.

According to Olive, and largely supported by memories related to me by John Warren and Kath Westcott, the Temperance movement in Hatherleigh was a strong social hub. Peter would join popular events and day trips organised for the many members. It was understood at the time that he enjoyed participating.

My mother, on the other hand, reported that my father had told her that he resented being coerced to join the movement and all its activities. An active social drinker during their marriage in later life, Mum blamed the Temperance movement for having caused unhappiness and rebellion in my father.

Whether rebellion against the Temperance movement, against school, against his overbearing family and small-town society, it is not entirely clear what motivated the young Peter. But one thing is for sure: he left the town in his teens to train as an aircraft engineer, then for national service, and finally for work around the UK and abroad, never to live in Hatherleigh again in his short life.

Chapter Three

Aden: Return Visits

Crater, 1996.

Bournemouth, 1996

The year was 1996 and I was in Bournemouth, UK to conduct an interview about my father. An old man and long retired, Jack had been my father's line manager at the South Yemen Air Force in Aden. He had lived two doors down from us in the airfield compound that housed the SYAF families.

399 Sloane Street was the house where we lived in the South Yemen Airforce compound in Aden.

Jack lived two doors away, to the rear of our house as it appears in this photo. Pamela, a woman that I discovered in 2018, and who I will write about later in this book, lived with her family just beyond him. The "White City" was named for its modernist white washed houses, which had been built in very stripped-down Art Deco style, with flat roofs and a mixture of typical Art Deco features of curved walls, metal-framed windows, portholes and other geometric shapes. There is some influence apparent here of the Bauhaus architecture of British Mandate Tel Aviv, designed by the refugee architects of the European Bauhaus school. These buildings were designed to be cool to an extent, and large windows and other features that would have been common in Europe would not have kept the buildings as cool as they could be. Air conditioning, as we know it, would not have been introduced until much later. Modernist housing, with these influences, was also increasingly used post-World War II in the UK and Europe for some British forces and other colonial accommodation. Modernist houses in Aden were relatively late colonial buildings, built as the colony grew in strategic importance and as a garrison in the early part of the 20th century. Aden had first been settled in 1839 as a bunkering port between Britain and its major colony of India. In those early days of colonial rule, it had been a province governed from Bombay and as such its earliest buildings had been constructed in colonial Indian style. These 19th century colonial buildings of India relied on high ceilings and verandahs to achieve maximum ventilation, but were not so effective at keeping buildings cool as windows let in heat, especially when south-facing. The streets of the White City were named for major London thoroughfares. Besides our own Sloane Street, I remember Park Lane and Regent Street. I believe there was also a Mayfair.

On a visit in late 1996 I managed to locate the Sloane Street house only after a determined search.

The former White City compound had lost its formidable perimeter fence and had been incorporated into the surrounding urban area on one side, whilst the airfield, which was still operational, remained to its rear. From the Khormaksar main drag I followed my instinct, negotiating dusty, rubbish strewn roads that wove through a hotchpotch of walled-in houses. In my mind I could still picture the grid of neatly swept streets, spaciously laid out and lined with white painted Art Deco houses, sparkling in the sun, that was my childhood air base home. And eventually I found the Sloane Street house. It was very early morning and all around me cheerful Adeni children were gathering to go to school. The girls wore short sleeved, white cotton dresses as I had done as a school child in my day in Aden. They all carried water bottles along with their school bags just as I remembered I had done. This part of the world is very hot and can be unbearably humid. School starts and ends early each day in order to avoid the searing afternoon heat. Personal water bottles are necessary accessories for thirsty school children in this climate. In order to obtain this photo of my old house I was allowed to climb onto the roof of a friendly neighbour's Land Cruiser, parked hard up against an imposing, wrought iron and barbed wire topped perimeter wall. The house was locked and empty. Its owner, I was informed, lived in another house on the coast. The upstairs room, where a strip light hangs from the window, was once my bedroom.

I could not remember him from those times, so listened in awe as Jack talked about knowing me as a girl, as well as my family and our home

Howa, our *ayah*, was Somali.

in Aden. He also remembered our *ayah* (a maid/nanny employed by the household) who had been friendly with his own *ayah*.

It had been traditional in colonial times for the British to employ Somali women as *ayahs* to look after children and carry out domestic duties.

These women had been following a well-travelled route across the Gulf of Aden from their homeland in the Horn of Africa in search of such work for generations. At independence in 1967, with the hasty withdrawal of thousands of British families, these women were suddenly left bereft and displaced far from their homeland. Directly after that event, we were amongst a rare few British families that were resident in Aden. All of us lived surrounded by high fences and barbed wire in our compound, where we were protected from post-independence trouble in the streets all around us. It was a daily routine that unemployed Somali *ayahs* would hang on the compound fences, begging to be given the only kind of job they knew from the only British people still in Aden. I personally remember those scenes well. Howa would have considered herself lucky to be chosen at the fence, and I remember her consolidating her position with us by taking care of us kids with great enthusiasm. We had fun times with her as she played with us, and sang Arabic nursery rhymes to us. Occasionally she would treat us to fresh popcorn, cooked on a brazier outside her *tukal*. (A *tukal* was a small building, usually to the rear of the main colonial house, where domestic staff would be quartered). My mother told me later in life that she had discovered from Howa that the former Somali *ayahs* who had not been lucky enough to find a family to work for had turned to prostitution to survive.

On the face of it having found such a closely placed source at the centre of my dad's world was an exciting development. As I listened to Jack recount his memories, I confidently expected to learn at least some detail about my father's mysterious disappearance in Aden.

However, whilst the old man talked to me about the type of person my dad was, being employed under him (aircraft maintenance with specialism in overseeing the workshops and the ordering and cataloguing of aircraft parts), and the Aden in which he had lived and worked, he could not tell me anything about what had ultimately happened to my dad.

In 1996 I incurred the wrath of anxious security guards when I snapped this photo of the gate
guardian at the airforce base where my father once worked.

The aeroplane depicted is an unidentified Russian aircraft, which would
have been put in place during Soviet-occupied Aden, the period which
followed Airwork's departure from the airfield. The base had originally
been built for the RAF during the time of British Aden. Prior to the 1967
departure of British forces from the Middle East at Aden's independence, a
Wing Commander John Severne was given a budget of two million pounds
by the British government to form a South Arabian Air Force at the base.
The operational commander and pilots of the new force were all British.
The aircraft arrived in August, September and October 1967. Airwork were
given a three-year contract to provide maintenance support, of which
my father was a part. Independence was declared on 30th November
1967 and the fledgling air force was immediately changed from the South
Arabian Air Force to the People's Democratic Republic of Yemen Air Force
(PDRYAF). Three months later, on 27th February 1968, all British personnel
were ordered to leave immediately, although Airwork staff was allowed to
stay until the end of their contract in 1970. When the Airwork contract was
finished, the government made moves towards a much closer collabora-
tion with the Soviet Union and Bulgaria. The PDRYAF received Soviet built

aircraft such as this gatekeeper. After unification of North and South Yemen in 1990, the joint Air Force operated a mixture of American and Russian equipment. There were internal problems within Yemen during the 1990s, and there has been fighting with Saudi Arabia more recently. The effect of all this conflict and upheaval on the air force has been that it has almost completely ceased to function.

Jack said that he had just left Aden for another posting when my father died in December 1969. He had heard of the incident only via the Airwork grapevine.

Meeting Jack was a bittersweet experience. On the one hand hearing snippets that I will treasure forever about a lost era of my dad's and my own life in Aden, but on the other hand to have my hopes of solving the lifelong mystery dashed. This was to prove the first disappointment amongst many.

Aden, 1996

A desire to find out more about my father had lain in the pit of my stomach like a troublesome dollop of expanding dough since the dark day we had been told, somewhat unconvincingly, that he had died. Instructed at that time not to talk to anyone about the little that I knew, much inside me had had been suppressed since childhood. By my early twenties a huge fermenting dough ball was close to exploding.

A conversation with my younger brother about the father we largely only knew from hushed remarks and innuendo that had surrounded us since childhood, had triggered my resolve to act. A years-long search that was to bounce me from agency to agency, geographical location to geographical location and between extremes of emotion, began to unravel from that moment.

Initial investigation saw me contact the former Airwork offices (by this time taken over by Bombardier Defence Services Ltd) at Hurn Airport in Dorset. Airwork had been the company that had seconded my father to the South Yemen Air Force in Aden. In 1996, staff in the Human Resources department at Hurn, remembering that their former employee had been in Aden, and still holding contact details for him, had referred me to Jack in Bournemouth.

In the end a broken reed in my search for hard facts about my dad, Jack did give me a fantastic lead that was to take me from, what had been until that time, a fledgling UK based search all the way to the heart of the matter in Aden.

Since doing national service in the 1950s, Jack had been a member of the Royal British Legion (RBL). Just before my arrival at his house he had spotted an advert for the RBL's first ever pilgrimage to Aden in his current copy of Legion Magazine.

Having been a British colony from 1839 to 1967, Aden houses two major graveyards of British subjects, many of them fallen servicemen. At the time I met Jack, there were many surviving family members in the UK wishing to visit the final resting place of loved ones that had died in the brutal conflict that raged in Aden in its final years under British rule in the 1960s. Almost without exception, these relatives had never before made the journey. Down the years Aden had either been too dangerous to visit or was a politically closed place, or both. In 1996 a small window of détente and opportunity had opened, and the British Legion were planning to take advantage of it.

Knowing that my family had been advised that my father had been buried at Ma'alla Christian Cemetery in Aden, Jack urged me to contact the RBL Pilgrimages department to see if I could join their trip. I worried at first because Dad was not only employed as a civilian worker in Aden, but also was there after the withdrawal of British forces, and I believed that I would not qualify, on either count, to join a services families' pilgrimage.

Happily, I could not have been more wrong. One phone call to their offices in Kent, and I was enthusiastically welcomed and signed up to join the RBL's first ever pilgrimage to Aden.

And so, very early on the morning of Monday 25th November 1996, I was amongst a group of 66 pilgrims aboard a Yemenia Airlines aircraft that touched down on the runway of Khormaksar Airport in Aden. Beside myself, the group included veterans of service, men and women, family members, widows, mothers and relatives. Whilst relieved to have arrived after a long and tiring journey from the UK, I was also nervous.

The two-year period that I had lived there from 1968–69, had seen the fall out of Britain's hasty and somewhat shambolic withdrawal from Aden in November 1967 having followed a prolonged period of terrorist uprising, strikes and general unrest in the colony. Whilst a great deal of the tension existed between local groups vying for position in the run up to independence, the violence and disorder had been primarily aimed at the colonial administration and the occupying military forces and their families.

My time as an impressionable young girl in Aden had therefore been spent in a maelstrom of hatred for, and malevolence against, my native

British people. I had also witnessed, first hand, the unravelling of local feuds and fighting after power and valuable infrastructure had been left behind at the withdrawal.

Those traumatic childhood memories made me fear the reception that we would receive as British visitors to Aden, and I was nervous about in what state I would find the place that I once called home.

Thus I emerged from the plane at Khormaksar early that morning wide-eyed and ready for anything. Having lived close to the airport in childhood, I was struck by the stiff monsoon breeze that came wafting across from surrounding salt flats. The humid smell of it was instantly and eerily familiar.

From there, the short bus trip to our hotel nearby was a journey back in time. Everything of the passing scenery I had seen before. It was as though the intervening years had stood still. Original colonial houses, buildings and general infrastructure remained with almost no new development to be seen anywhere. The only aspect that marked the passing of time since I had last come this way in 1969 was that absolutely everything was damaged, either by wear and tear, or by the ravages of civil war and strife.

Once we arrived there, however, our hotel turned out to be a brand new edifice. Built on recently reclaimed land adjacent to the main road that I had once travelled along every day to and from school, it stood where I had back then seen only an expanse of shallow sea dotted with pink blobs of wading flamingos. Tall, flat fronted and glass-plated, the hotel was a mirage of modernity rising out of low level, ramshackle Khormaksar. From my balcony I could see the panorama of Aden. Situated on a peninsula that hangs from the southwest coast of Yemen into the Gulf of Aden, between the Red Sea and the Indian Ocean, Aden is especially notable for its wide, deep water harbour and a jagged, grey volcanic skyline. My first sight of those two starkly beautiful natural phenomena that morning was both breathtaking and comforting. There could be no more poignant a reminder that I was back in Aden.

Tired as we all were, our RBL leaders lost no time in launching us on our schedule. There were visits for each of us to old haunts. I saw the temporary apartment block that had housed us when I first arrived in Aden in January 1968, then our house where Jack had been our neighbour, my school and various other familiar places of my childhood. Most importantly we were taken to Aden's two British cemeteries to visit the graves of our loved ones. First there was a familiarisation visit, then, at the end of the trip, there were remembrance services at both. But this was where I was to face my next disappointment.

Back in the UK, in the run up to the pilgrimage, I was phoned at home by one of the RBL organisers. I knew at once from his faltering voice that Gerry had something difficult he had to tell me. I thought perhaps the trip might have been cancelled. Instead, the news that Gerry had to deliver to me was simultaneously shocking whilst not entirely unexpected.

Gerry had received advance intelligence from on the ground in Aden (the RBL were dealing with both Mustapha, the Adeni born British consul and Nadir, a locally born British officer of the British Federal Regular Army, who had special responsibility for the British graveyards left behind in Aden). He had been informed that no grave existed, or had ever existed, for my father in Ma'alla Christian Cemetery, where my family had been informed that he had been buried.

Files and records had been destroyed during Aden's long period of civil war and strife since Dad had died in 1969. But Nadir had been keeping his own records since independence and had none for Peter Balkwill. He had also paced the graveyard himself to check for a headstone that he might have missed, Gerry had told me.

So it was that I landed up on our visit to Ma'alla Christian Cemetery amongst a group of pilgrims visiting the resting place of their loved ones, with no grave of my own to visit.

The general mood that afternoon was understandably subdued. The cemetery was set in an arid, urban landscape, dominated on one side by peeling, dilapidated blocks of flats and on the other by huge rusting fuel storage tanks. The ground was volcanic and acacia trees dotted about provided only patchy shade. There were tears from grieving relatives, and a haunting wail from a mother who was visiting for the first time the grave of a still born child that she had given birth to over thirty years previously.

As for me, Gerry asked me to select one of the many unmarked graves that populate this cemetery, which had been ransacked and damaged through Aden's long period of strife. He then produced a cross, homemade in oak by the RBL and bearing my father's name and date of death. We then planted the cross and a chaplain said prayers over it. It was a poignant moment and I cried a lot. My tears were less for the loss of my family's loved one, but for all of our lives that might have been, had he come home to us instead of disappearing in Aden.

This official pilgrimage visit to Aden was both a milestone in the history of Britain's involvement with its one-time colony, as well being a historic occasion for me.

The Royal British Legion had led the first official contingent of returning servicemen and women, and civilians and their families since independence, 29 years previously. It had been a high profile trip and we had variously been escorted by British Consulate and Embassy staff, the British military attaché to the Middle East, religious leaders, medical staff, local dignitaries and local police. There had been receptions in our honour, and a remembrance service for our dead loved ones. We had been taken on personal tours the length and breadth of Aden and the surrounding territory. We had humbling experiences as we met local people who recognised their former colonial masters for who they were, but had welcomed us cheerfully, such was the period of détente in Aden at that time.

For me, however, the end of this trip signalled unfinished business. I was to return to Aden two more times, in 1997 and 1998, to try to find out more about what had really happened to my dad.

Planting a cross for Dad. Ma'alla Christian Cemetery, November 1996.

Aden Revisits

At Tarshayn.

1996

Naturally, given the mystery that had been deepening since I had begun my research about my father's death, I took the opportunity to carry out, alongside my interaction with the official pilgrimage itinerary, an "on the ground" investigation into what might have happened to my father.

As mentioned above, I had been phoned at home in the days before we were due to leave for Aden by a RBL official, who had regretted to inform me that my father's grave had not been found in the Ma'alla Christian Cemetery. Extensive investigations had been made by experienced people who I was later to meet, and not only could a grave not be found, but no record of one either.

I was given the option to drop out of the trip because of this, but I chose to continue. Having begun tentative enquiries from the UK, I saw the RBL trip as my chance to investigate further and more thoroughly. Besides, I longed to revisit a place of my childhood.

My experience with the other pilgrims was harrowing. And my own story was to register its particular emotional toll. However, getting the chance to see Aden again and learn more about the place and circumstances in which I had formerly lived, as well as beginning my enquiries, was extremely positive. I am glad I took the decision to remain with the group.

And so, I began my on-the-spot investigation in which I was assisted no end by the Deputy Ambassador, British Consul, Defence Attaché, the retired Adeni Federal Regular Army officer and local people in my search.

With FRA officer, Ali Nadir, I scoured the Christian graveyards of Aden, plus one Muslim one, to try to see if we could find a relevant headstone, or clues, anywhere. With the help of Mustapha, the British Consul, an official British Embassy record of my father's death was eventually found. It had been entered into a ledger, which had, at some point down the years, been removed from Aden and was being stored at the then British Embassy in Sana'a. Hospital records were searched for (it had been reported to us in 1969 that he had died from a head wound at the Queen Elizabeth Hospital in the Crater district of Aden, known by 1996 as the Al Ghamooria Hospital) but could not be found. It was the same story with newspaper archives. Local Adenis asked around the senior members of their families who would have been old enough to remember December 1969. The only information that came back from that initiative was that one old man thought he remembered the accident being reported on the radio at the time, but no specific details.

A chance visit to Aziz Bookshop at Steamer Point brought an emotional, though ultimately unproductive, surprise. At that time of 1996, this bookshop was well known as a time warp of a place, and so quite a curiosity. It was for that reason that a few of us from the pilgrimage popped in there. The old soldiers who accompanied me remembered that they would shop there during their 1960s postings in Aden.

For them, entering via the solid, blue painted doorway into the fusty interior of the shop was a step back in time. I remember them gasping as they saw cabinets and shelves still stocked with goods instantly recognisable from their yester years; Mr Aziz himself, standing behind a glass topped counter beaming at them, as if they had never been away.

As the guys perused affectionately the selection of post cards, albums, stationery and magazines that were so familiar to them, I took the opportunity to show Mr Aziz a photograph of my father.

Now it was the turn of the old shopkeeper to become misty-eyed with memories. About the same age as my dad would have been, Mr Aziz recalled that Dad, and what seems to have been his Airwork colleagues, would drop into the shop to collect British newspapers that he would order in for them. It would be quite the event of the week for them, he told me, as they looked forward to catching up with news from home. Apparently, they would take their papers to the bar of the nearby Sailors Mission to read at leisure. He described the men as a group: long shirts worn loose over beige shorts, sunglasses in breast pockets, dark socks and fuzzy mosquito boots. This certainly rang true of my dad and the men that I remembered.

But Mr Aziz had only known my dad as a customer. He was not aware of the fate that had subsequently befallen him in Aden, and had no useful information about him for me.

Nevertheless, it was heart-warming for me to talk to a person about what would almost certainly have been one of the last sightings of my dad. Our group left the shop happily, the guys with handfuls of retro purchases, and me with the warm glow of a renewed memory.

Mr Aziz watched us go, shaking his head thoughtfully, a trace of a smile on his face, as he remembered the British, and the days when the colony, and the port that they had built, bustled. It was the glorious time that his shop had prospered and his life was good. He recalled, no doubt, with fondness the last of the British expat workers, such as my dad, who stayed on after independence. They had been the very last customers, some quarter of a century previous to this meeting, who had had any call for the merchandise of his now long since stagnant shop.

1997

Exactly a year after my first revisit to Aden, I was given the opportunity to visit again. The British Legion was to be running a second Remembrance Day pilgrimage.

Arrangements by them were much the same as before, and the personalities connected with the running of the trip also remained. I was able to reconnect with people who knew about the story of my dad who were willing to continue to help me in my search to find out what had happened to him. To that end various meetings were set up for me with local people to see if they might know of anything significant.

I attended a seafood banquet hosted by a prominent business family in the Little Aden area. Although I had an enjoyable time and sampled some of the very fine seafood dishes for which the south of Yemen is known, nobody present, despite having been well connected in Aden at the time of my dad's death, could come up with any useful information.

I then went to a cricket match organised by members of the Indian community in Aden. There were just a few of them left by the 1990s, as most had left at independence to start businesses anew in more prosperous parts of the globe, such as the United Arab Emirates (UAE). That was fun too, if a bit wistful. Sitting in the empty rows of seats of a once fine stadium that would have teemed with spectators. Watching the handful of men left in Aden that knew and cared about the sport still slogging it out on a bedraggled pitch, I could see in their happy faces the love they still felt for the game. But no one from the Indian community remembered my dad either.

Then came a bombshell break through. A guest from the fish banquet had subsequently discovered that a friend of his not only remembered my dad but had been our next door neighbour at the White City.

I personally remembered Fouad. A telephone call was set up between us and I spoke to him from my hotel room. He was unwilling to meet me face to face but talked cheerfully to me on the phone. He remembered particularly fondly that I used to play with his son when we were children living next door to each other. I did indeed remember Mohammed, a mild-mannered boy with eyes like black olives.

Although it was a pleasant chat I could gain no positive new news from Fouad. Instead he threw a series of curve balls, which disrupted completely the official Airwork version of how my father died which I had been living with for nearly thirty years. He told me that my dad had been trying to cross the Ma'alla dual carriageway whilst drunk when he was struck by a car. And he told me that the reason I could not find a grave was that my father had actually been cremated. Fouad was very clear about this despite me pointing out to him that the widow (my mother) had been informed by letter sent to the UK that he had been buried in Ma'alla Christian Cemetery. Aside from going on to confirm to me something that my mother had once told me, which is that my dad had been run down by a colleague and neighbour, who he then named as Farouk Hassan Ali, Fouad did not want to talk further and he terminated our conversation.

1998

I left Aden soon after the 1997 phone call, disappointed but vowing to return. A year later, I found myself in Aden once again, this time on a small, privately arranged trip.

Perhaps because having already run two trips, the British Legion was now finding it difficult to attract any further interest in their pilgrimages. Or perhaps because, following the long-awaited détente that had allowed them to make those first visits to the troubled place that Aden had long been, they sensed that the recent window of a stable security situation was now changing. Whatever the reason, the RBL had declined to run a third pilgrimage trip in 1998.

So a group of interested people put our heads together and achieved the somewhat difficult task of getting ourselves out to Aden for a third occasion. For the others, all veterans of service in Aden, the trip was entirely recreational. I saw it, however, as a possible opportunity to continue to pursue my investigation.

In the event we had a very enjoyable time. Accepted into the hearts of the Adenis who had been getting to know us over the past couple of years, we were invited to visit all kinds of places. In particular, I visited my old convent school, now an Islamic girls school, where I was cheerfully welcomed by the pupils. We went to a football tournament. We even got involved in learning to belly dance in our hotel's nightclub.

However, despite my pleasant trip, I sadly could find no further information about my father. Try as I might, I could not raise Fouad again to answer a myriad questions I had thought of since I had last spoken to him.

The editor of Al Ayyam, the local Aden newspaper, was summoned and he and I penned an article together, appealing for anyone who might know anything about Peter Balkwill, or his accident in 1969, to come forward. But nothing at all came of that and I left Aden with a heavy heart.

It turned out that the British Legion had been spot on if it had indeed been the case earlier that they considered that the security situation in Yemen was changing for the worse.

On 29th December 1998, a matter of only about a month since my visit to Aden that year, a group of Western tourists were being driven along an open plain towards Aden in a convoy of Toyota Land Cruisers. They had been sightseeing in the Yemeni interior. At noon on that fateful day, they were attacked by a group of approximately 20 men, armed with bazookas, rocket-propelled grenades and Kalashnikov rifles. The gang kidnapped the tourists and then drove them for some 20 minutes to a desert ravine. There the highly agitated kidnappers abused their hostages. The Westerners had been targeted, it seemed, because they were considered to be "infidels".

After about 24 hours a large-scale rescue operation, involving more than 200 troops, was launched by the Yemeni government. Chaos ensued. Guns were fired and grenades were thrown. Some of the tourists were used by the kidnappers as human shields. By the end of that day three hostages — two women and one man — lay dead. Others were seriously injured.

This event seems to have been the result of an early Al Qaeda operation in Yemen. It signalled a downturn of the security situation in the country, which has, for all kinds of reasons, continued to worsen to this day.

It is therefore unlikely that I will travel again to Aden any time soon.

Boy from the Moor

Chapter Four

Impressions of Aden

Elephant Bay, Aden

The place called Aden where Peter, The Boy from the Moor, met his end, and where I went to search for him, is also a place that has meant many things to many different people. Its evolving population including over the years Yemenis, both southern and northern, economic migrants from places such as Somalia and Ethiopia and far flung sub continental India, as well as Lebanese, Italians and Greeks and so on. Travellers and writers came, such as Freya Stark and Evelyn Waugh. Day trippers from liners docked at the port, and the crews of foreign cargo ships from all parts of the world visited. The colonial British elite as well as civilian professionals who between them ensured the running of the place also, of course, came to live. And then there were the thousands of military personnel from all the forces, and their families, who occupied the once enormous garrison of British Aden.

A home, a posting, a professional challenge, a business opportunity, a tourist spot, a shopper's paradise, Aden has been all of these things to so many people. The peninsula suspended in the Gulf of Aden from the South Yemen's southern tip, with the Red Sea just around the corner and the Indian Ocean just down the gulf. There are natural wonders in Aden: a volcano, an extraordinary climate, a long, beautiful coastline and deep waters, an exotic blend of cultures and, all around, the remaining vestiges of a mix of the people and their systems that have held sway in the area throughout history.

Contained in this chapter is just a small collection of some impressions of Aden that will be familiar to the many people who have inhabited or visited there.

This unidentified photo, which must have been taken in the earliest times of Aden Colony, is almost certainly of what used to be called Signal Hill. The mast was used for communications with the ships in the harbour below. Situated beyond the areas of Steamer Point and Tawahi, the British Governor's Residence and the British Embassy were here. I remember enjoying children's Christmas parties at the Embassy during my time in Aden, and my parents attending receptions there. As members of a very small British expat community, our family tended to be on the invite list in one way or another! I understand that after we left in 1969, the embassy was moved to residential Khormaksar, into what was possibly our very own Sloane Street.

This photo, from my parents' collection, is dated 1968 and was taken from what was then called Tarshayn Beach, in the area of Telegraph Hill. When my family first arrived in 1968, Tarshayn was an abandoned beach club which had served the British forces families during the occupation. We would enjoy our Friday rest day (Muslim holy day) each week at that deserted place up until the surrounding shark nets, seen as a symbol of the hated recent British presence in Aden, were cut during a night of unrest. Having been a thriving port until that time, sharks were a persistent threat to swimmers in Adeni waters. We therefore had to move to a beach club with secure netting for our protection from sharks. During my 1996 visit, I learned from locals that sharks left the area after independence as a result of the demise of the harbour, as there were no longer the flotsam and jetsam of food scraps from ships. Private enquiries have revealed that Tarshayn became known as Russian Beach after the population that arrived in what had become, by then, Communist Aden. They had taken over the former beach club and availed themselves of the facilities there. It is now Sahel al-Aroosah, meaning Bride Beach in Arabic, and is a holiday resort known as Arosa.

In 1996 the Prince of Wales Pier, pictured here, stood as solid as when it had been built in 1919, but was by now redundant and abandoned. It had been built at Steamer Point in Tawahi, near the entrance to Aden Harbour. The Suez Canal was opened in 1869, speeding up the shipping route from Britain via the Mediterranean and the Red Sea, and cutting short the previously long route that had traditionally been followed around the southern tip of Africa. Thanks to this, Aden found itself an important strategic transit port en route to India, the Far East and Australia. Generations of passengers, during the long era of liner travel, passed through the Prince of Wales tourist terminal. Aden had by that time become a world centre for trade, duty-free shopping and tourism. The port of Aden and its commercial centre then all but died, with the twin events of 1967 of the closure of the Suez Canal due to war between Egypt and Israel, and the withdrawal of the British from Aden. At the time of writing in 2019, and following four years of a bitter civil war, the Prince of Wales Pier stands, in common with much of the infrastructure of Aden, in abandoned ruins.

This 1960s view from Aden Harbour shows Steamer Point, where liners would dock at the Prince of Wales Pier. Immediately behind lies the shopping area of Tawahi, where disembarking passengers would head to buy duty-free goods from around the world, such as china, cameras and state-of-the-art electrical goods from Japan, pearls from other parts of the Middle East and watches and perfume from Europe. They might then take a taxi from The Crescent at Tawahi to the district of Crater where higgledy-piggledy streets were lined with gold and jewellery merchants. In the background of this picture rise the iconic volcanic peaks of the Aden peninsula. Legend has it that if you climb Mount Shamsan, the highest point in the range, then you will never return to Aden.

This 1996 view across the slopes of Ma'alla shows modern day Ummul Island in the harbour beyond. Known during colonial times as Slave Island, British military equipment that was left behind at the 1967 withdrawal was dumped there.

The Ma'alla Straight, pictured here, was, at the time it was built, and still was when I saw it in 1996, a fast dual carriageway road connecting Khormaksar to Steamer Point and Tawahi. In this 1960s view, traffic travels on the left-hand side, according to British tradition. By the time of my revisit in 1996, and after a long occupation of Aden by countries of the Communist bloc, vehicles were being driven on the right-hand side. I was told during my 1996 visit that Ma'alla stands on land that was reclaimed at some stage during the British occupation. There are apartment blocks to one side of the carriageway backing onto the harbour behind, and on the other side standing in front of the foothills of the volcanic slopes of the peninsula's interior. At the time this photo was taken, British families were occupying these apartments (note the British red pillar box at the corner of the second block in the picture). By the time I was travelling this route from home to school and back between the years of 1968 and 1969, families from around Yemen that were moving into Aden immediately after its independence were beginning to move into these buildings. In many cases, I understand this was a land grab, and from my seat on the school bus I personally witnessed overcrowding in these apartments and a rapid decline of the fabric of the buildings. On a personal note, my family was informed that my father was killed by a speeding car as he attempted to cross the road from a cold store shop.

This scene shows Crater, circa 1960s. Featuring apartments and buildings used by British families, it gives an aura of spaciousness and order. In reality Crater is what it says it is; a district of Aden built within an extinct volcano crater. As such, it is closed in by geographical boundaries of rock and sea. Throughout British rule Crater remained a traditional home of Yemenis and other ethnic groups. Winding alleys of Arabic homes, shops and cafes, and bustling *souks* (market places), teeming with local life, existed hard up in restricted space against Western-style, British developments. With the terror campaign against the British in the final years of their rule in Aden, which would have been from around the time this photo was taken, Crater became a melting pot of tension and violence. Given the hotch-potch conditions people were living in, and the fact that dissenting Yemenis, including within the Federal Army — a force comprised of local soldiers, who based themselves there, it became impossible for the British to distinguish Arab friend from Arab foe. A mutiny and ambushes in June 1967 by the Federal Army and local police that signaled the final decline of the British in Aden happened in Crater. I was told by ex-British servicemen on the 1996 Aden pilgrimage that, in the chaotic last few months up to that point, British forces, in response to terror attacks on their personnel and families, developed an undercover operation, largely concentrated in Crater. The Keeni Meeni (from the Swahili word for "sneaky") squad comprised of men specially trained in hand-to-hand, urban combat who would enter the area in disguise, often, I was told, dressed in women's traditional burqas. Accompanying a British soldier in uniform who acted as a stalking horse, the Keeni Meenis would identify and neutralise would-be assassins amongst the crowds.

This Mosque of Abu Bakr al-Aydarus, or Aidrus Mosque, in Aidrus Street, symbolises for me the ethnic roots of Crater. It is a Sufi mosque, named for Abu Bakr al-Aydarus, the *wali* or "patron saint" of Aden. It was originally built in the late 15th or early 16th century and underwent rebuilding after being destroyed in 1859. Further damage was inflicted during Yemen's 1994 civil war, but today the mosque still stands. Abu Bakr al-Aydarus was born in Tarim in the Hadhramaut Valley of south Yemen and was a scholar of Sufism, the mystical branch of Islam. He led most of his adult life in Aden, where he was a missionary, and where he oversaw the construction of the mosque that bears his name. He was so well respected by the city's residents for his good work that he was later made the *wali* of Aden.

In an act of personal history, I pose for a photo in Crater. As the two years that I lived in Aden as a child were during the chaotic period immediately following independence, I was subject to many rules and restrictions imposed on my people for our safety. As we were British, it was feared that we would be seen as symbols of former British oppression in Aden, and could easily become targets of violence and assassination. During the colony's final years, immediately before our arrival, Crater had become a hotbed of violence and terror in the area, atrocities against the British having both been planned and carried out in Crater by freedom fighters based there. The Crater area was deemed to be still too unsafe during our time for us to enter, and so I never went there as a child. As most of the *souks* were situated in Crater, my mother would send our *ayah*, Howa, in to buy the things that we needed. As a Somali, Howa would have been immune from the threat we would have faced. By 1996 however, it became apparent when I entered Crater accompanied by retired former British soldiers who had done national service as young men in Aden, that bygones had become bygones. Local people who we came across there were mostly too young to have ever met a British person, since our presence had been so very absent during the long years since the withdrawal, and looked on us with gentle curiosity. The older generation, we were surprised to find, recognising absolutely my companions for the occupying soldiers that they had once been, came up and personally welcomed us with emotion. They had, it seemed, felt that they had suffered more hardship in the intervening years of Communism and civil war than they ever remembered under British rule. My military companions had their own emotional memories connected with Crater. As ex members of the Royal Northumberland (RN) Fusiliers, they were attending the 1996 pilgrimage in order to honour comrades from their regiment that had been killed in a day of uprising and ambushes in Crater. On that day in June 1967, members of the Federal Army, a force of locally recruited men, mutinied and turned on their British colleagues of the RN Fusiliers and other regiments, and 22 men were killed. In turn British control of Crater, at the heart of Aden, was lost. This event was to lead to a historic re-taking of, and reestablishment of control of, Crater by the Argyll and Sutherland Highlanders under the command of Lt Col Mike Mitchell, which they kept until the final withdrawal later that year. Nicknamed "Mad Mitch" by British journalists reporting out of Aden, Lt Col Mitchell was a maverick who operated against instructions and with an infamous iron grip on the situation in Crater. At the time my father was working unaccompanied in Aden, in advance of the arrival of my mother, brother and I joining him there. I clearly remember as a six-year-old child, adults discussing distress-ing headlines that filled the press about "Mad Mitch" and the situation in Aden at home in the UK with my mother. There was worry for my dad who was living amongst it. And, knowing that we were scheduled to join him after independence, worry for what we all might face in the future in Aden.

Chapter Five

National Service

January 11th 1946, Airman 3077641

As the story of *Boy from the Moor* unfolds it will reveal a complex mystery and the intricate personality of its central character, Peter Balkwill. As my dad died whilst I was only eight years old, the character I present here has been built up mostly by research I have carried out over the past 25 years. An overall account, I believe, will present a picture of the man that took himself to a place, in circumstances where he would disappear almost without trace. Along with my own personal memories and talking extensively to friends and colleagues of my dad, I feel that his experience of national service was a major factor that drove him to seek the kind of lifestyle he went on to adopt. So, I am devoting this chapter of *Boy from the Moor* to what I have come to learn about Dad's time "in the service".

National service was already defunct by the time I was a small child. I certainly never knew of it, or Dad's role in it, whilst he was alive, and it has taken time and consideration following my research to comprehend the impact this short, intense period had on him.

National service was a system of compulsory or voluntary government conscription usually military. Typically, it required all male citizens to enrol for up to two years, usually at age 18. National service existed in the UK from 1916 to 1920, and then again from 1939 to 1960, covering all three branches of the military.

My father's Royal Air Force Service and Release Book, shown here, reveals that he served between 11th January 1946 and 26th January 1948. His service number was 3077641.

It has been possible to learn a little from this Service and Release book about young Peter. For instance, he is listed as being 5'10" at the time of entry. A "statement of special aptitudes or qualities or any special types of employment for which recommended" at the time of his release notes: "A rather quiet somewhat shy

Service and Release Book, 1946–1948.

airman, tends to give the impression that he knows little or nothing. In actual fact he is a most dependable and thorough tradesman who can be relied upon always." Receipts for encashment of postal drafts following his release reveal his initial movements after leaving. The first two are in Okehampton, confirming what I have been told, that he returned immediately home to Devon. The next is in Southampton. The final stamp, of April 1948, is in Chichester. I have never established what he was doing in the latter two south coast cities of the UK, but assume that it was a return to a career that he had already established before RAF service in civilian aviation in those locations. He had, I had been told by folk in his hometown of Hatherleigh, trained from age 16 as an airframe fitter at Shebbear College, cross country to the north of the town, where he apparently boarded. Peter had always been, in common with many boys of his generation, mad keen on aeroplanes.

So how was I able to build up a picture of the experiences of Airman 3077641 Peter J Balkwill and the impact they might have had on his personality? Well, I spoke to three of his peers. First, his boyhood friend John Warren, who did his RAF service alongside him. Second, a friend, Jack Clark, who never knew him, but who did his Army service stationed close by in Egypt, and has memories of visiting John and Dad's air base there. And third, my Uncle Alan, my mother's brother, who knew him personally. Alan entered RAF service in 1948, just as Peter was leaving.

The essential facts were established with John and his wife, Marianne. The couple, who knew my dad from their youth, shared their memories about a dear friend they cherished. I only took sketchy notes then, and as John and Marianne have both since passed away I have not been able to return for clarification.

I am not clear whether John and Peter trained together. My dad's Service and Release Book shows that he began his service at RAF Kirkham in Lancashire. However, they did then travel together, according to John, to spend the major part of their national service at Camp Fayid air station in the Suez Canal zone of Egypt. The Service and Release Book lists Peter's overseas service as being from 20th September 1946 to 26th January 1948.

Working on the Lockheed Lodestar in Egypt.

John recounted vividly their time in Egypt. The camaraderie, with the boys from Devon palling up with lads from all around the UK. In particular John and Peter became friendly with a Welshman who answered, somewhat predictably, to the name of Taff. A nickname that the friends apparently coined for my dad was, according to John, "Flash". Coming to grips with the alien environment of a desert camp in a foreign country far from home, the men lived in tents, ate in canteens, bathed in wash blocks and socialised, always together and almost always on camp. There was a strict RAF hierarchy that oversaw their entire existence, there were daily interactions with Arab speaking locals, and women were scarce. National service caused the lads both joy and sadness: appreciation of their coming of age and self-discovery, but also grief and hardship, as they made this huge foray into an outside world that they had never before known. John told me Taff was tragically murdered. Picked off by a Fedayeen sniper, who aimed his rifle through a narrow, semi-open wash block window. The presence of British troops in Upper Egypt in the late 1940s, I understand, was to protect the Suez Canal zone, a vital waterway for transport around the British Empire. The Fedayeen, the name deriving from the classical Arabic *fidayin*, the singular of which, *fidai*, means "one who gives his life for another or for a cause," were local assassins opposed to occupation. As well as the British presence in Suez, they were also against the newly created state of Israel.

That era in Egypt also saw the stirrings of Gamal Abdel Nasser's revolution of 1952, which overthrew the sitting Egyptian royal family, signalling a long campaign by the new leader Nasser for pan-Arab nationalism, and an end to British colonial rule throughout the Middle East. Seemingly Taff had become an early casualty of the Arab nationalist cause. John told me that the tragedy had a profound and lasting effect on Peter, who was standing at the next washbasin to Taff as they shaved together. Dad's great friend had fallen dead beside him, shot in the head, without him even understanding what on earth had happened. The Egyptian marksman, John told me, had slipped away and was never caught, he had been that efficient.

Camp Life.

Also emotionally challenging for that group of RAF airmen, John said, was that they were issued rifles and given the brief to guard the remaining German prisoners of war of the North African campaign, essentially granting the RAF lads authority over their peers. John talked of the enormity of the realisation that the defeated enemy was made up of human beings just like themselves. In a rare moment of insightful comment about my dad, my mum once spoke of him confiding in her the helplessness that he had felt at being so young whilst assuming responsibility over another man's life, and how brutal it had felt to hold that rifle. John told me that he and my dad had particular empathy for one German prisoner, who John was still corresponding with at the time of our meeting in 2002.

Speaking to my friend, Jack, in recent years it transpired that he did his service with the Army in Tel el Kebir, Egypt. This British army station was not far from the RAF base at Al Fayid in the Suez Canal zone. Indeed, Jack remembers making an overnight visit to Al Fayid with Army supplies. As he did service from 1947 (touchingly he recalls vividly that he enrolled on the wedding day of Queen Elizabeth II and Phillip, 20th November of that year), it seems that he would have been there around the time my father was leaving.

As John Warren had done before him, Jack recounted his national service days in Egypt enthusiastically to me, echoing similar sentiments. Additionally, Jack has a knack for recognising small yet significant details. He related cameo sketches that brought camp life alive in that place at that time. These memories have contributed to an understanding of how my father might have felt in Egypt, and the lasting impression that this military service would have had on him there.

Jack recalls sand as being the overwhelming enemy. When the desert wind got up, fine granules of displaced sand would get everywhere; into clothing, bedding, food and especially exposed bums on wash block toilet seats, a huge irritant in the confined and basic lives of the British squaddies.

Petty theft could also be a problem, particularly of boots from tents. But he remembers no animosity from the locals at Tel el Kebir at all, such as the terror incident that killed Taff at Fayid. Indeed Jack remembers fondly working with cheerful Egyptian staff in the Army tool sheds and getting to know them and their customs. He particularly remembers a Muslim colleague who happily used the excuse of working with Westerners to avoid joining in the Ramadan fast of that year.

His visit to Dad's RAF camp was an eye opener for Jack. Entering Al Fayid after a "smashing run" through the desert to deliver lorry spare parts from his Army base, he was struck by the orderliness of the place compared to his own camp. He particularly remembers the brightly white washed rocks that neatly demarcated roadways of brushed sand. He passed a cinema where he saw RAF lads escorting WRAFs (Women's Royal Air Force) from a film. Where there were few women on camp at Fayid, there were none at all at Tel el Kebir, and Jack envied this snapshot of regular life. He felt that the RAF lads had a "cushier time of it" than the Army boys. But he enjoyed his overnight stay with them at Al Fayid nonetheless.

Both Jack and John remembered their journeys home as adventures. They each travelled by troop ship from Port Said. The ships were converted 1930s passenger liners of the type that had been used to ferry emigrants from the UK to the New World up until the 1930s. Marianne Warren remembered the "joyous day" the Hatherleigh women gathered in the town square to welcome home their cohort of lads, who arrived by bus from the boat.

Finally, I interviewed my Uncle Alan. He spoke about both his service with the RAF and also of having known my dad personally.

Sitting across from him as he recounted his memories, I was struck by him expressing happily wistful emotions similar to those I saw on the face of John, and Jack, that I had interviewed before him. Now in his late 80s, Alan remains mentally alert, and no more so than when talking about service days. Without pausing to reflect, he rattled off to me his service number (2394128), and the locations he was sent to; Padgate to be kitted out, RAF West Kirby for "square bashing", i.e. military drill, Melksham for eight weeks of training and finally RAF Leeming, Yorkshire, where he worked on Mosquito aircraft until demobilisation. Alan remembered his medical, and even the sum sent to him by postal order at call up to buy toiletries and essentials for his forthcoming trip: five shillings (25 pence in today's money).

Whilst I had hoped to learn from my uncle a little about his enlistment into the RAF (he talked of "going where I was put", which was for training as an electrical assistant), as it would have been similar to my dad's Air Force induction a couple of years earlier, Alan believed that Dad's experience had been a different one. The two clues that made him say this were that the dates in Dad's service book show he started out relatively late at aged over 19, whereas Alan and Jack began at 18, and that his service number was unusual. Where Alan and everybody he knew had a number beginning with a two, Dad's number was 3077641. His Service and Release Book was blue whereas Alan's was a buff colour. It is uncertain the reason for these discrepancies, but Alan suspects that Dad's dedicated training in Devon was the cause, and that he may have volunteered rather than been conscripted. Dad would likely have opted for deferred entry, which would have allowed him to finish training for his skill, which in turn would have allowed him to follow his trade in the service rather than being placed "where he was put" as had happened to my uncle. Marianne had told me years before that Dad's main RAF role had been "rigger and inspection", which, Alan pointed out to me, lies within the remit of Dad's trade as an airframe fitter.

Alan then spoke a little about how he had felt at demob and his return to life in "civvy street". He felt that he had "entered as a boy, but had grown up quickly." He had emerged from the experience "a different person." He had learned a trade and discipline. He had come to learn that life "was an adventure that would take you as far as you were prepared to go." He relished that he had met young men from all parts of the country and all walks of life. Some of these were to become friends for life. Indeed, a service pal acted as his best man at his subsequent wedding. He also spoke of happily reuniting with his childhood friends who had had their own experiences. His best friend Ken had gone into the Army. Another friend John, a farmworker, had been exempt from serving. Farming was considered essential work, and a "reserve occupation" as World War II had just ended in 1945, and the industry was required to assist in the drive to revive and increase food production following the lean war years. John stayed to assist his father run the family farm, but other brothers were conscripted as it was a "one son at home" policy, Alan explained.

At the close of our interview, my Uncle Alan chatted briefly about what he knew personally of my father. It was a short interlude as Alan never got the chance to know my dad well.

Alan and Joan's home city is Cambridge, which situated in the east of the UK, is quite a stretch from Dad's childhood home in the moors of Devon, in the far southwest of the country. In those days, roads between the two were basic, and journey times were long. Added to that, Dad was often away anyway, working all over the country and abroad in his job with aircraft.

Peter and Joan had met after his national service in 1950, in a pub in her local village whilst he was working at an airfield near Cambridge.

Alan remembers his brother-in-law as a somewhat enigmatic figure, four years older than him and eight years older than Joan, a stranger from a distant part of the country, worldly and detached. He admired Peter. Peter owned a Renault car, in which he came to collect Joan for evenings out. Alan could only dream of owning a car in those days. Peter was qualified in aircraft and regularly employed by some of the cutting-edge companies in the industry of the day. As a keen aeroplane fan Alan remembers, for instance, being impressed that Peter worked at Bourn Helicopters (now Bond Helicopters), Marshalls of Cambridge, and in the fledgling post war crop spraying business.

Alan also remembers that Peter had a sophisticated sense of humour. When Peter discovered that Joan's brother enjoyed playing elementary tunes on the family piano, he persuaded Joan to show Alan a photo of her new boyfriend. The photo was actually of a big band leader. Believing that Peter was a professional and fashionable musician, Alan became nervous about his own basic piano skills.

When the two men finally met face-to-face at a family tea, Alan was very relieved to find that Joan's new boyfriend was not a big band leader after all.

Alan was impressed by the audacity of the joke, and how he was taken in by it. Alan recalls the day in 1969 that he visited his parents and was given the shock news that Peter had been killed in Aden. He was offered no explanation as to what had happened, and he didn't ask. Those were the days of "making do" and "getting on with it".

In common with John and Jack, Alan chose to return to his home area and capitalise on all that he had learnt during national service. John became a shop owner in south Devon. Jack returned to the Midlands and became an engineer in a factory. Alan meanwhile went back to Cambridge, and after a spell in the accounts department of the Co-Op, became a successful publican.

However, Peter seemed to choose to use his service experience as the launch pad for the itinerant and adventurous life style that ultimately led to his early demise.

Boy from the Moor

Chapter Six

Band of Brothers in Aden

1968: The Airwork guys enjoy their
Christmas lunch. Peter is seated
halfway down on the right, looking
towards the camera.

My first arrival in Aden as an innocent six-year-old was an experience I will never forget. In this chapter, I'll talk about it to illustrate what I saw then, and what I remember from those days that helped me come to understand the legacy that national service had on my father.

Dad went to work for the South Arabian Air Force (SAAF) in Aden at the start of 1967. The SAAF was being founded in Aden as the air force of the new South Yemen at a time when plans were taking shape for the colony's independence from British rule. The British staff of this air force was seconded there by the Bournemouth-based firm, Airwork. I have heard on the grapevine that a core group of these guys had been recruited from an RAF base in Cambridgeshire. My dad on the other hand made his way to Aden to follow a friend from his Sudan days (where we had formerly lived). Unlike the RAF guys, Dad's only military experience to date had been national service. He had been in civilian employment in the aircraft industry in the intervening years before going to work in this air force of another country.

The header photo to this chapter shows the Airwork staff Christmas lunch, 1968, which was a year after independence in Aden, and two years into Peter's contract.

In those early days of the SAAF (which would become the People's Democratic Republic of Yemen Air Force after independence) the Airwork men were unaccompanied. Aden was still a colony and the British services, the diplomatic corps and civilian expats were all still present. The Airwork men had to wait for the housing occupied by these people to be vacated at the British withdrawal before they could bring their own families over to live in the newly vacated homes.

Thus, we arrived in early 1968 to join the men. A fractious independence had occurred a couple of months previously, earlier than scheduled due to a hasty British withdrawal following a series of disastrous events in the colony. Until then the Airwork men had been based at the British RAF station, living in the mess there, which was in the Khormaksar district of Aden, and was scheduled for handover to the new South Yemen government at independence.

These men had arrived in a situation that, whilst tense, was tentatively stable. They were surrounded in Aden by British colonial expats still living a privileged and interesting lifestyle. Occasionally they interacted with that community, although they were always based together at Khormaksar. As conditions deteriorated in Aden and its surrounds, they continued to work and reside at the airfield and most were present through the chaotic and frightening night that was independence on 30th November 1967.

Years after the event, and after the personal trauma of Aden that my mother was harbouring had begun to subside, Mum told me some of what Dad had told her of that night.

The married men had each been issued an unoccupied apartment on an RAF residential compound named Dhobi Lines, and a rifle. They were to spend that night, in what was to become their new family home, protecting this property from a feared land grab in Aden by Yemenis who might swarm in from the countryside, Mum said. Dad told her that it was only the second time in his life that he had held a rifle, national service, some 20 years previously, being the first. He was terrified, he said, and dreaded what was to come.

As tracer fire lit up the night sky, he cowered as intermittent blazing light burst in via the cracks of closed shutters, and bounced in narrow beams about the walls of the bare apartment. And he heard a cacophony of chaos exploding all around as he sat alone, rifle ready, in his empty home. Windows were shuttered and doors sealed in case of sniper fire.

Now that I have assimilated his whole life story, I can begin to imagine how overwhelming it must have been reliving twin terrible events from service experience in Egypt: amid enormous danger, he toted his rifle, in charge not only of the situation around him, but also of his own survival. All of this must have made guarding a hapless captured soldier in Egypt, pale by comparison. The threat of death by sniper fire in an unlikely domestic setting, as had happened to his national service pal Taff in the wash block at Camp Fayid, must have had him plumbing the depths of unimaginably torrid emotions.

Nevertheless, Dad and the others emerged unscathed and blinking at the light of dawn into an Aden smouldering from the firestorm of the night before. Camaraderie, exposure to adversity and how to deal with it, and a sense of "making do and getting on with it", instilled at an early age by national service, must, I feel, have been what got all of those men through that extraordinarily difficult time.

The Dhobi Lines compound was engulfed by a heavy-duty iron fence. A further fortification of a snake of hooped barbed wire lay at its foot, on the surrounding waste ground of volcanic sand. Perhaps this metallic assault course is what saved the men from attack that night. These formidable defences were still in place when I arrived about five weeks later. They occupied my imagination daily as I lived and played on the air base, wondering at this awesome barrier that stood intractably separating me from the world outside.

Dhobi Lines compound. (The formidable perimeter fence not visible in this photo).

At six years old I had never been in a military environment before. My life had until then revolved around the genteel existence of our home in a villa in early post-colonial Sudan, and annual holidays in the Edwardian households of both sets of my grandparents in the UK.

Within the compound I would see Dad and our neighbours, who were also his colleagues and friends, behaving as if being penned in was normal daily activity. For them, I realise now, this way of living and working was merely an extension of life on a national service camp. They just forgot to explain that to the children that had come to live alongside them in Aden.

Dhobi Lines was a temporary first home for us in Aden. After a few months all the families moved into a second fenced-in airbase compound named the White City. This was a step up for us as accommodation there was former RAF officers' quarters, as opposed to the prefabricated wooden apartment blocks of the rank and file that we had been living in.

But Dhobi Lines will remain always my crash course introduction to daily life in Aden in the aftermath of independence.

In keeping with a long-held tradition of Britain's hottest colonies, Airwork staff would work from first light until midday, when the sun was burning at its height making working conditions barely tolerable. Their school age children kept similar hours. Thus, families would reunite in their compound homes for lunch, after which the parents would retire to sleep off the afternoon torpor. Not so their children. Young and still brimming with energy, the afternoons would be alive with possibility for us unsupervised kids.

Daily we roamed as a gang within the confines of the Dhobi Lines compound, where a trove of remarkable things lay in jumbled abandonment by the people who had lived there before us. Inside some apartments that had remained uninhabited by Airwork families, we found rooms that were, Marie Celeste-like, filled with belongings that had been left behind in the hasty withdrawal. There would have been some women and children here. We found colourful packets of products, recognisable from back in the UK; foodstuffs, washing powder and cleaning products, and remains of sets of crockery and utensils in the kitchens. I particularly remember tin openers, so many tin openers. Within the plasterboard wooden walls of living rooms and bedrooms, we found toys. There must have been a craze for playing marbles amongst the service children of British Aden, as we found the colourful glass balls, in varying sizes, everywhere in the compound. Not just inside, but also outside, nestling in the volcanic dirt and sparkling attractively in the light of the strong afternoon sun. We would collect them and marbles became a kind of a currency within our childhood group. Overwhelmingly though, the personal articles left behind seemed to be men's belongings. I remember white tiled bathrooms, peeling and rusting and infested with cockroaches, strewn with Old Spice men's grooming products. This popular 1960s brand, its logo of a white galleon depicted on a pillar box red background, is forever synonymous for me with those empty Aden flats, and an overwhelming aura I sensed of masculinity about the place.

Out in the compound we kids could only stare in wonderment and envy at a children's play area of swings, see-saws and climbing frames, similar to what we had enjoyed back in recreation grounds in the UK. Inexplicably to us, this playground had been fenced off by thorny coils of the ubiquitous barbed wire and we could not reach it. So it stood there, brimming with possibility for us yet starkly alone and unused.

On my 1996 return visit to Aden with the Royal British Legion, I learned from fellow travellers that had been soldiers serving in Aden at the time of the British withdrawal, that the Dhobi Lines compound had, with its proximity to the airstrip, played a pivotal role in the British evacuation of

1967. When Sir Humphrey Trevelyan, the last High Commissioner of Aden and the Federation of South Arabia and his staff departed on the final day, the last remaining troops secured their departure.

A particular story told to me by a former Royal Engineer resonated. This man said that he had been based at Sheikh Othman alongside the Parachute Regiment. The Sheikh Othman district lies to the far side of the air force base to the airstrip and the Dhobi Lines compound at Khormaksar. Along with the Royal Marines, who had been the first troops to arrive in Aden in 1839, these men were the last to leave the ground in Aden at independence. He talked about the retreat following the evacuation of civilians, service families and important pieces of infrastructure. This was the retreat of the last remaining troops from throughout the colony to the air base perimeter, in readiness for the final airlift. At Sheikh Othman, he, of course, was already in place on one side. But it was his belief that other troops took up positions in the Dhobi Lines flats on the Khormaksar side in the final days of making ready for the departure. It was awe inspiring for me in the mid-1990s to discover that it was the legacy of these men that had left messy bathrooms full of their toiletries. Also to discover the nature of their mission, which had necessitated so much barbed wire in a seemingly inappropriate setting, that I had been struggling to make sense of since childhood in Aden 30 years before. And this story illustrated for me, overwhelmingly, the eye of the storm my father endured at Dhobi Lines that fearful night of withdrawal on 30th November 1967.

The Royal Engineer told me his own story of yomping from Sheikh Othman across the air base to helicopters waiting to depart on the airstrip. The event he described was the culmination of intense activity in Aden in the last days of the withdrawal, focused on the Dhobi Lines. Alongside evacuation of personnel, important and valuable articles were lifted in nets from the airfield and transferred to ships waiting in Aden harbour. I spoke with an elderly widow of a former RAF chef. She remembered the moment industrial fridges of meat were being air lifted, and a net broke. Hundreds of cuts of pork rained down on Khormaksar, causing agitation amid the Muslim community there. It was a crazy time, she said. And I thought to myself that my dad must have witnessed it all.

Those very last marines and engineers were the ones who guarded the departure of the High Commissioner from Aden. He was taken by helicopter from the airstrip to the warship HMS Intrepid which was waiting in the harbour, from where he was, I believe, transferred to Bahrain. By all accounts, there was just a little ceremony as Sir Humphrey Trevelyan left. Merely a brass band playing "Fings Ain't Wot They Used to Be", as he boarded the helicopter, its blades whirring, then rotating faster and faster until he was lifted up and away into the bright Arabian sky.

No doubt my dad, who I remember as a music lover and follower of popular culture whilst in the UK, would have heard and recognised the tune as brassy strains, borne on a flat breeze, reached his ears at the Dhobi Lines, from the instruments on the airfield. "Fings Ain't Wot They Used to Be" was a musical comedy about low life characters in Soho in the 1950s. It was a well-known production in its day. Quite what its relevance to the final departure of the British from Aden that historic day was, I can only guess. Maybe the song title was an allusion to the end of the Empire and its tradition after well over 100 years.

The song, however, speaks humorously of a Britain that was modernising. I have a mental picture of my dad and the guys stationed in their Dhobi Lines apartments, as heat and danger crackled in the air around them. They are musing on familiar lyrics: "Teds with drain pipe trousers", "beer was frothy, now it's frothy coffee" and "monkeys flying round the moon, we'll be up there soon". Lyrics that reminded them of a brighter, shinier way of life that they knew of, but which lay across the miles of desert, where their loved ones and homes that they could only dream of lay.

1968. Airwork fielded a cricket team against BP refinery workers at Little Aden.

Not all of the Airwork men were accompanied. There were young bachelors and unaccompanied family men too. This wide-ranging group tended to gravitate around the married families, looking for normalcy away from their own homes.

Joining in Family Life. An Airwork engineer relaxes at our house.

And so it was that I found myself, along with my family in near constant masculine company in Aden. Our home was a hub for men in the loose khaki shirts and shorts, mosquito boots and Ray Ban sunglasses that were their work wear in the intense Aden heat. They would arrive from the airfield in military style open topped Jeeps. Set against the vista of the neatly marked, sandy roadway outside our home, as Jack had described the roads to be at Al Fayid RAF camp in Egypt, I was reminded of this scene as a teenager later in the UK, watching the American TV show M*A*S*H, which was about army camp hospital life in the Korean war of 1950–1953.

The guys seemed happy, joining us for special occasions and accompanying us on outings on our weekly Friday day off.

A regular communal Friday beach trip.

Doing everything together and making their own fun was, I personally recall, the hallmark of this generation of men, for whom the common bond was that they had all set out in life as young national service conscripts or volunteers.

Boy from the Moor

Chapter Seven

Love Story

Courting days. At Grand Parade,
Skegness, early 1950s.

My mum, Joan, was 16 when her father tipped her the wink that there was an evening job going at the pub in their village.

A second job washing glasses behind the bar, as she was legally too young to serve at the pumps, would give her extra pocket money. A recent school leaver, Joan's new day job was in a high-end fashion store in nearby Cambridge. She loved fashion and each day at the store, surrounded by the latest clothing styles, felt more like a day in fashion dream world than work to her. Extra pennies earned at the pub were going to come in handy to save up, with the help of staff discount, to buy some wonderful clothes.

These were happy times for Mum. Whereas she would refuse to talk to me about the stress of living in Aden and the pain of losing my dad, memories she shared of earlier times as a lively teenager fizzed with enthusiasm. I almost felt that I was living the experience with her.

And so, I know that one evening in 1950, when Mum was at her sink in the pub, her father sitting among the locals at the bar, a familiar crowd of young aircraft engineers from nearby Bourn airfield (my dad, I believe, was working at that time for Pest Control, based at Bourn) entered the smoky, beer-smelling room.

But there was one guy in the group that she had never seen before. That stranger was dark haired and broad faced, with a dimple in his cheek. He had olive skin and deep brown eyes. My mum thought, with such unusually dark good looks, that he must be a foreigner.

Peter Balkwill might well have been a foreigner. Joan had spent her whole life in the East Anglia area of the UK, and she knew about as much of Peter's moorland homeland in the deep southwest of the country as she would have done about anywhere abroad.

It was no coincidence that Peter came into the pub that night. Travelling for work (I understand that his job at the airfield involved work on helicopters for the crop spraying industry), Peter was rooming in a boarding house in the Chesterton area of Cambridge. He was lonely and he was shy. Despite his good looks and friendly personality, he found it difficult to relate to women. His workmates, having previously spotted Joan in the pub, thought her the perfect girl for him. They were right. A love affair followed.

Happy times in the garden of the pub where they met: Peter and Joan (right hand side) and friends. 1950s.

At 24 Peter was eight years older than Joan. It was to turn out that the maturity and worldly experience that he could bring to their relationship would be matched by a youthful vitality and charm on her part, as well as an irresistible lack of guile. They both had a work ethic and a desire to get on in life. Each was a product of their era and liked to live the experiences of their youth to the full. Where he was rooted in the time of the early 20th century, of jazz and big bands, of black and white cinema, of Edwardian Revival jackets and waist coats and tapered trousers and slick hair styles, of dining in corner houses with white table cloths, she was all about the flamboyant 1950s of rock and roll music, dancing and roller skating, of drinking frothy coffee in shiny cafes. There was both common and uncommon ground for the pair to bond over. Plus Joan's father approved of Peter. This came as a relief, since he had already dismissed a succession of American airmen out of hand.

Cambridgeshire, and nearby Suffolk, had become home to several American air bases during World War II. With the subsequent onset of the Cold War the bases had then remained. Nightlife in the centre of Cambridge at that time was filled with young American servicemen enjoying time off. The spirit of excitement and adventure that they brought proved intoxicating to the local female population.

But there was always resentment, and, for some reason, a hint of scandal around liaisons formed between American airmen and local girls in the community. And my granddad, for one, would not stand for his only daughter being involved with "some damn Yank."

During the war, Mum's teenage aunt, a woman she was close with, had met and married an officer of the Free Czechoslovak Army that had been stationed in their village. Having grown up alongside her, Mum had lived and breathed her aunt's adventures. Mum dreamed that she too would someday meet a dashing foreigner.

Her chances with handsome (they were all handsome, I have seen the photos!) American airmen were all scuppered by her father, so the arrival of my dad, of whom Granddad heartily approved, was her dream come true.

The necessity for a long courtship (Peter and Joan were to be finally married six years later) was twofold. Firstly, they needed to save money. Prospects at that post-war time were not immediate. At the same time as saving towards a home for themselves (and indeed they spent some of their early married years living in a caravan), Peter was also sending remittances to his parents, who struggled for survival in Devon, following World War I. The other reason was that Joan was so very young. Peter apparently told her, as well as her parents, to whom he became very quickly close, that he needed to "wait for you/her to grow up."

And so Peter set himself up as a mentor for Joan. He quickly raised her social expectations with dates in restaurants. Unused, at that time to eating anything other than home cooked food, waiter service and the gradual introduction, following the war, of foreign food to British menus, eating out was a revelation to young Joan.

He would also take her to the cinema. On one occasion, that she fondly recalled from time to time, he took her to see "Tell Your Children". This is an American church propaganda film, originally released in 1936, so already vintage by that time. It is a melodramatic story, revolving around the perils of marijuana use by young people, intended to be shown to parents as a morality tale, attempting to teach them about the dangers of cannabis use. The film has subsequently been renamed "Reefer Madness" and remains in the public domain today, having gained new life as an unintentional satire among advocates of cannabis policy reform.

Mum was already a heavy nicotine smoker by the time she met Dad. She had started at age 14. She hoped to emulate the glamour of Hollywood stars of the day, who were atmospherically filmed and photographed drawing moodily on cigarettes. At that time, and in the circles she moved in, cigarette smoking was socially acceptable, and the dangers of nicotine use were largely unknown. For Mum, her cigarette habit sufficed, and she had no intention of experimenting further. Dad, however, who did not smoke at all, and considered himself to be the more worldly wise of the two of them, worried that her habit could make Joan susceptible to the perceived danger of cannabis use. She liked to poke gentle fun, as she would describe to me in her later years, at the earnestness with which he took her along to "Tell Your Children" as another one of her early life lessons.

But at the same time Peter was also to push Joan's boundaries and lead her to racy adventures both at home and abroad. According to Mum, Dad would take her from Cambridge by train on trips to Soho in London. Dad considered himself to be fashionable. He was careful about his appearance and his image. He liked to follow popular music.

Their visits would revolve around a trip to Cecil Gee in Long Acre, which Peter considered to be the most fashionable of men's outfitters of the day. Then on to Denmark Street to buy the New Musical Express, a recently founded, cutting edge music publication. Quite why he had to collect his copy direct from the publishers (Denmark Street was considered to be London's version of New York's "Tin Pan Alley", where music shops, studios and music publishers were concentrated) is unknown, but it is clear that he was a man who kept a finger on the pulse of every one of his interests.

Dad's business at hand dealt with, the rest of the day and evening, until the last train back to Cambridge from King's Cross, would be free to spend wandering the streets and alleyways of Soho. Fashionable coffee bars and music venues that they liked to frequent existed there, cheek by jowl, among town houses, pubs, strip clubs and clip joints. Peter and Joan warmed to the thrill of the area's energetic vibe and counter cultural current. The red lights of prostitutes' doorbells, however, were ever present and Joan was shocked, she later told me, when, on more than once occasion, Peter, walking arm in arm with her, was brazenly approached by women touting for their trade. Peter's early adventures with Joan were opening her eyes wide to a bigger and more vibrant world than anything she had ever before known, where he intended to take her to live with him.

Peter and Joan married one blustery March day in 1956. The church was but a walk across the road from her parents' house. Friends and her family attended, but his relatives were unable to make the journey from Devon. Both her wedding suit and "going away" outfit were purchased from the store where she worked; monochrome padded shouldered jackets and pinched waist skirts, all Hollywood cinematic glamour. She declined a bouquet to carry an ivory coloured bible, sporting instead, as a single splash of colour, a corsage of freesias on her lapel. After a homemade reception, the couple left by train for London to spend their honeymoon enjoying themselves in Soho, of course. Their hotel was one that Peter knew of at nearby Victoria. In those days there was an air terminal in Buckingham Palace Road, to and from which buses would ferry air passengers from the fast-developing airport out at Heathrow to make their onward connections. He knew of The Eccleston Hotel from his international travels. I have toured the area in the present day trying to locate the two buildings. I was unsuccessful with the hotel, though I did spot "The Airways Hotel" in St Georges Drive, near Victoria Rail Station, which surely is a throwback to the days when there was a connection with air travel in the area. The former air terminal is now the National Audit Office, and is an impressive Art Deco-style building.

29th March 1956, Peter and Joan married in the church opposite her house near Cambridge.

Joan had never before stayed in a hotel or spent a night with Peter. She recounted to me many times her embarrassment as they stood in front of the receptionist on arrival at The Eccleston Hotel, dotted with confetti, just waiting to get upstairs together.

Peter travelled extensively for work during his courtship and marriage with Joan. He was fond of sending notes to her back at home, scribbled on the back of post cards of the many places he visited. Most of these snatched messages reveal a character wistful for home and company there.

THE GRAND HOTEL, KHARTOUM

TROPICAL PHOTO STORES
KARAKASHIAN BROS.
KHARTOUM

After five years of marriage, Peter and Joan moved to Khartoum to live. In 1960 he sent this post card to her at the address of a caravan park in Cambridgeshire, where they had spent several years of their married life to that date. Seemingly, from his message on the back of the card, he had gone ahead of her to Sudan, a country he knew well from having already worked there for several years in the crop spraying industry, to begin a job with Sudan Airways. His words to her are enthusiastic and fill the entire message space of the card. He is clearly looking forward to their future in Khartoum and has been making all kinds of arrangements for them there. Joan was already pregnant with me (her first child) when she arrived to join him some months later.

Greetings from Aden

In 1966 Peter's job in Sudan reached a natural end. Joan and the children (I had been joined in 1965 by my brother, Peter junior) moved back to Cambridge. Peter then went to work in Aden in the run up to independence from Britain there. During that time Aden was in increasing turmoil, which was heavily reported in the newspapers back in the UK. I remember Mum fretting the entire year until we went to join him in Aden in January 1968. I will never forget the day during that time that Mum received a parcel in the post from Aden. It contained a jewel-encrusted brooch in the shape of a *jambiya* (customary Yemeni dagger) and a note from him assuring her that all would be well and begging her to join him. He then sent this Christmas card home to us in December 1967. His words inside the card simply read: "Have one for me!!! Love to all". The image on the card is of the old colonial Crescent Hotel, Tawahi, Aden. By early January we were in Aden, living with him.

From Cheltenham, during the early days of their courtship. He complains that her last letter "wasn't much", that he has had laryngitis, and that it "makes you drink!!!"

From Corsica in 1953, en route, with a pilot flying a crop sprayer light aircraft, to Sudan from the UK for a season of spraying cotton in the south of the country. He complains: "Corsica — the place they send all the people they want to get rid of" and "Couldn't find a fish and chip shop in Lyon last night so had to make do with a steak."

Following on from the above, this one from Tunis: "As you can see they set me "free" from Corsica after all. No fish and chip shops here — please forward some of "them pies.""

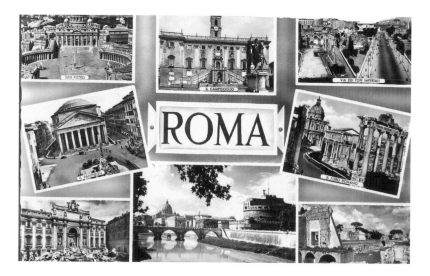

After their marriage, he sent this one to their address at the Cambridge-shire caravan park, in which he complains "... only wish I could see the town/city or whatever it is."

Chapter Eight

Gypsy Crop Sprayer

Ground equipment work with Pest
Control in Cambridgeshire.

My mum told me that she met my dad in 1950 when he was employed by a firm called Pest Control at a Cambridge airfield. This is the earliest record I have of him working in aerial crop spraying.

I understand he received aircraft fitter training, aged 16, in 1942, going on to do national service with the RAF, specialising in "rigger and inspection" until 1948. I have no idea at all at what point he first entered the business of crop spraying. Nor did I know anything, aside from casual observations made by Mum about her courtship with him whilst he was a crop sprayer, about his career in that industry. Until, that is, I began my research into his life and death.

Crop spraying (or crop dusting) is defined as "the spraying of powdered insecticide or liquid on crops, especially from the air".

I managed to track down two friends of Dad's who, whilst they did not work with him in crop spraying, met him later on in his aviation career and knew some details about that time of his life and about that line of work.

Alan met my dad in 1960 when they both worked at Sudan Airways in Khartoum, shortly after Dad had left crop spraying. Ted, younger than Dad by about ten years, met him when he arrived in Sudan, also in 1960, to join a new generation of crop sprayers working on the Gezira cotton scheme, some 200 miles south of Khartoum, where Dad had been employed a decade earlier. I had known both of these men as a child in Sudan and it was very exciting to discover them again, and to hear what they had to say about my father.

What they both revealed was a man of two characters. On the one hand, a maverick who chose not to live amongst Khartoum's expat community in the modern "New Quarter" of the city, but in an old colonial villa set in grounds at Mogran, sandwiched between the university and a zoo. On the other hand, a dedicated "Englishman", maintaining strong links with his home country and surrounding himself with English food, knick knacks and tradition when in Khartoum. As well as being sociable and hospitable, along with my mother, entertaining a wide circle of friends, from Brits and Westerners to Armenians, Greeks and Ethiopians and local Sudanese associates, in the comfort of the Mogran house, he could also be a loner. Alan went as far as to describe him as "a man with a difference", and, with affection, "an oddball". With Joan alongside, Peter also managed to mix family life and serious friendships, not least among the Muslim and British diplomatic communities, with a heady expatriate lifestyle that pulsated around them in the heat and dust of those early post-colonial days in Khartoum.

As he had been acquainted with the Gezira crop sprayers working in Sudan at the time he was there in the early 1960s, Alan believed their lifestyle, which my dad had lived before them, was the one that will enduringly define Dad's character.

The Gezira Scheme is an irrigation project centred on the state of Al Jazirah, meaning "island" in Arabic, just southeast of the confluence of the Blue and White Nile rivers, below Khartoum.

The Gezira Scheme was initially financed by the Sudan Plantations Syndicate in London. Later, the British government guaranteed capital to develop it. Then the Sudan Gezira Board took over in 1950.

It was originally envisaged that wheat would be grown in the region. But that plan was abandoned in favour of Egyptian-type long staple cotton. Cotton was first grown in the area in 1904, then further developed in 1914. In modern times cotton is still the main crop grown in Gezira.

Alan told me that Pest Control, under the direction of a character well-known throughout Sudan by the name of Ladi Marmol, had been the company responsible for cotton spraying in Gezira from Dad's time with them in the 1950s until his own time in Sudan ten years later.

Pest Control was the company my dad worked for in Cambridge in 1950. I came to learn from Alan that they also had outfits in Lincolnshire, in Boston and Skegness. This would explain tales my mother told of day trips from Cambridge to Skegness to visit Dad, and a pile of old black and white photos she left behind of him, and them both, there.

Skegness, April 1954. This photo was taken at a time when Peter was working on the annual maintenance of the Sudan crop spraying aircraft in Lincolnshire, U.K.

WEDNESDAY, NOVEMBER 11,

HUNT FOR BRITONS IN LOST PLANE

" Star " Reporter

RESCUE planes today searched for an Auster aircraft with two British flyers which disappeared over the Mediterranean between Tunis and Sardinia.

The pilot is Mr John Teasdale and with him his is his mechanic, Mr Ernest Thomas.

They were flying a plane belonging to Aerial Spraying Contractors, of Boston, Lincolnshire back to England from the Sudan, where they had been spraying cotton plantations.

Two other planes belonging to the same company were flying back at the same time.

They landed at Cagliari, Sardinia, and reported that the third plane disappeared about 60 miles south of Sardinia.

Rescue planes were sent out, but saw no trace of ths missing Auster. One of them, a seaplane, had engine trouble and spent several hours afloat on the sea before taking off again.

Alan explained that the light aircraft used for spraying in Sudan would be flown down there from Lincolnshire each cotton season, which would be the closing months of each year. This was typically a journey of 3,200 miles, being completed in 34 flying hours, spread over ten days. The spraying concluded, the aircraft would then be flown back to the UK for maintenance. A team of a pilot with an aircraft engineer was responsible for each aeroplane. My father was one of those engineers, and he would send post cards home to my mum, whom he was courting at the time, from each of his ports of call on the long journeys between UK and Sudan.

From Le Touquet to Cannes, Livorno, Tangier and Tunis, Dad's post cards, arriving in cold, drab 1950s England, would likely have seemed exotic. The reality was that this was a tough, dangerous (at least one aircraft was lost in the Mediterranean between Tunis and Sardinia in 1953) and quite lonely job.

In 1953, returning the crop spraying aircraft to Lincolnshire from Sudan, one of the planes was suddenly lost at sea. Peter was at the time flying in one of the two accompanying planes mentioned in this article, and survived the journey.

94

Alan referred to the men, and in particular my dad, who carried out this work, as being like "migrating birds" and "unaccompanied gypsies". They "were a roving band, who all knew each other".

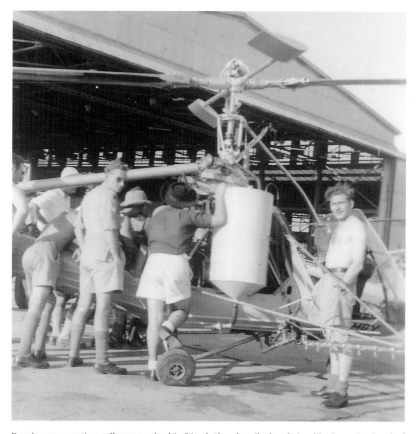

Peter's crop spraying colleagues, who his friend Alan described as being like "a roving band of gypsies" seen here working on a Hiller helicopter.

Once in the workplace, Gezira life was to get a whole lot more unglamorous. Almost certainly during Dad's time, the men lived in tents, sleeping under mosquito nets outside.

Food was basic and local. There was a requirement to get on with local, Arabic speaking employees. It was in Gezira, Alan believed, that Dad perfected the language, having begun to pick it up during national service in Egypt. He was a fluent speaker by the time he died 15 years later.

The work could be dangerous. The planes could and did crash for a number of reasons. As the aircraft were obliged to fly low over the crops that they sprayed, a particular hazard both in Sudan and the UK were telegraph wires, which could bring down a plane and maim its occupants. Dangerous chemicals were routinely handled by the crop sprayers. In particular my dad worked with DDT, a synthetic compound used as an insecticide, which replaced nicotine insecticide in the early 1950s. They were spraying against cotton jassid, an insect, which lives and feeds entirely on the undersides of the leaves of the cotton plant, which proved difficult to spray from the air.

Here a local man has been employed to act as a marker for the pilot to judge the area of cotton to be sprayed. He is reclining perilously close to the plane's toxic trail at a time when the dangers of working with the chemical DDT were not as well known as they are today.

Alan said he felt that his itinerant lifestyle in the Middle East, beginning with national service in Egypt, was not only the hallmark of my Dad, but a natural legacy of his solitary childhood existence on the wide open countryside, below the big skies of the moor in Devon. Being a part of the "roving band" of "gypsies" working, not only in crop spraying, but in all branches of aviation in that part of the world, following World War II, was close to everything he knew and was a comfort to him. Furthermore, Alan told me that he felt that Dad had always been happiest when working on small aircraft, being more conducive to travel and adventure, and working with like-minded souls. Apparently, when Dad joined Sudan Airways to work as an engineer, he became very unhappy at working on large passenger aircraft in an environment he considered impersonal.

The solution he found to this problem was to relocate to the airline's tool sheds, where he worked happily with local Sudanese staff on the equipment, which serviced the modest Sudan Airways fleet of the day. In summary, Alan said that he was not at all surprised that the *Boy from the Moor* chose to continue making his life in aviation in the Middle East, ultimately in Aden where he was to meet his demise.

Peter titled this photo "All mod cons". The British crop sprayers worked alongside local people on the cotton spraying scheme.

As an aside, I remember clearly as a six-year-old girl, having just arrived with my family to join Dad in Aden, him showing me excitedly around the area that I had come to live in. A stop on his tour was a spot near the airfield where he worked where stood, somewhat incongruously and all alone, a cotton bush. His enthusiasm when he showed me this lone plant was so heightened that I have never forgotten it. At a time when I was so very young I knew vaguely that my dad had once had something to do with cotton, but not the full, fascinating story of his time as a Gezira crop sprayer. Years later I was to learn that there had been a cotton scheme set up in the early 1950s in Abyan, formerly a part of the Fadhli sultanate (the moment the People's Republic of South Yemen had been established the previous November, all local statelets had been dissolved), to the east of Aden, noted for its agriculture. And I wonder, to this day, if Dad's excitement about the cotton bush, and about Aden in general, was that he might, in time, find a use for his skills that might keep him in the area in his future life. Aden had been booming for decades, with a world class harbour and a thriving duty-free trade. At that turning point time of independence from Britain, my dad could not have known whether or not Aden would end up following the successful models of other former British port cities such as Dubai and Singapore, and I guess he hoped it would.

Ted Weinel not only personally knew my dad in Sudan, but as a former engineer on the Gezira project, has been able to share his observations about Dad's character and to describe to me the type of work which he would have undertaken in Gezira. Ted went to work on the scheme some ten years after my dad had started, at a time when Dad had moved on to Sudan Airways in Khartoum.

Ever since I had learned that Dad's specialism in the RAF had been "rigger and inspection", the trade of aircraft fitter, I had wondered what the term actually meant. It was Ted that explained this to me. And as he told me that crop spraying aeroplanes were often old light aircraft modified for use in spraying, I came to understand why Dad's trade was so useful in the crop spraying industry.

Ted told me that "rigger" was a common title used by the Royal Flying Corps, Royal Air Force and the early Fleet Air Arm for one who "rigs" the "rigging" of aeroplanes, as they were then. In those times aircraft were often called "string bags" because they were built of wood with metal fittings and covered with tightened canvas. Most were biplanes and both wings and fuselages were stressed against flexing by using rigging-wires set diagonally opposed within the body structure and/or between the fuselage, the wings and wing struts separating the wings. Those between the wings were usually streamlined and called landing wires and flying wires, depending upon their physical and dynamic function when in place. Thus, the title of "rigger "was applied to those airmen who were qualified to adjust the so-called "rigging", interference with which could seriously affect flight characteristics.

This is a Tiger Moth plane flying over a cotton plantation. The Tiger Moth is a perfect example of aircraft "rigging".

Ted has kindly written a piece for inclusion here about his own time on the Gezira cotton project, which is the closest I can possibly get to knowing what my father's life as a crop sprayer in Sudan might have been like.

Ted's Account:

After a short period with my new aviation employer's headquarter base on the Isle of Wight, I was sent to the Sudan with a technical team in support of Four brand new Piper Super Cub aircraft, which had been converted for long range flight and crop spraying operations. I had helped with the conversion work along with another engineer, Trevor Young who, by then, had already become a good friend.

The day after our own arrival in the Sudan, Trevor and I set about preparing for the arrival of the aircraft after their long ferry flight from the UK. We had travelled by a regular BOAC flight from London in the company of four other company fellows, two entomologists and two airstrip supervisors, arriving one early morning in the Sudan's capital, Khartoum. This was my very first excursion to work overseas out of the UK, and my first impressions were of heat and the very exciting smell of Africa, lasting impressions that remain with me even now and even after the many new adventures abroad, thereafter.

The company's contract was seasonal, an annual arrangement governed by the cotton planting and six to seven month growth time.

There were several aviation companies who had won similar contractual obligations, since cotton growing in the triangle formed by the two Niles and their confluence at Khartoum (called Al Jazirah) was very extensive. Thousands upon thousands of acres were husbanded in that huge zone, being irrigated by a system of canals drawing water from the Sennar dam on the Blue Nile in the south. There were also hundreds of smaller government and privately owned cotton schemes up and down the banks of both rivers. The whole of Al Jazirah was, by then, owned and farmed by the Sudanese Government.

The four Pipers were scheduled to arrive in a few days' time, and preparation for spraying would start. Meanwhile the contract manager and a licensed chief engineer had joined us along with four young Sudanese aircraft fitters to swell the ranks of our company's presence in the country. Contract planning and manpower distribution was soon in full swing.

There were to be three bases of operation in the south for the duration of the 1961 spray season. One on the Blue Nile at Sennar, the main base on the White Nile at Kosti, and the last also on the White Nile at Ed Dueim. All were south of the capital in the cotton growing area of those times. However, all the company's contractual work was to be conducted only on smaller government and private schemes. These were called "pump schemes" because water for the irrigation of cultivated areas was drawn from the rivers using diesel powered pump systems, unlike the Gezira region which was watered by two huge canals and sub canal systems drawing water from the Blue Nile at the Sennar dam. The canal system had a long history dating back to late Victorian times under the then colonial rule.

I was delegated to work at Ed Dueim with one pilot and his aeroplane. Trevor would be sent to Sennar with his pilot and aircraft, whilst the Kosti base would be served by two aircraft with their respective pilots and strip supervisors. Kosti, being the main base, was both the organisational and aircraft maintenance centre for the whole of the company's operations in the Sudan.

At location the aircraft were to be served by teams of locally employed crews manning chemical tanker units. These people would be controlled by the strip supervisors on location, as they moved around the region of operation to use improvised airstrips located near the contracted cotton schemes. Likewise, each base had its own entomologists and commercial managers who would be contracting and implementing the spraying activity. Equally, each base would carry a small mess in which would live

Latterly the Gezira crop sprayers lodged in rented accommodation. During his time there in earlier years however, Peter lived at this camp and slept outside at night under a mosquito net. The photo is dated 1953.

the pilots, engineers, entomologists and commercial control fellows. A "mess" staff of cook and houseboy would look after household chores.

In seasons past, living in the field was under canvas, using ex-military tents. However, those days were gone and the subsidiary company had rented suitable fixed accommodation in the form of houses at each base. Simple furnishings and equipment were transported down to each accommodation in readiness for the start of the spraying season.

– Ted Weinel, Denia, 30th July 2017

Boy from the Moor

Chapter Nine

Last Heydays

Father Christmas arrives
at The Sudan Club.

The photo on the previous page shows Father Christmas arriving at the Sudan Airways staff children's Christmas party. It was 1965 and I was four years old. I clearly remember my father excitedly taking me to the "aircraft" that Father Christmas had emerged from. In reality it was a Land Rover that had been rigged with sheeting and decorated with the airline's livery. My father and his ground crew team had been responsible for the makeover. It must have taken them many hours. For expatriates, those days in Khartoum were long and they had the luxury of a great deal of leisure time. The social life was extensive and there were many opportunities for hobbies and leisure activities. I remember it as a privileged and happy time.

In 1960 British Prime Minister Harold Macmillan made a month-long trip to Africa. Concurrently my father, Peter Balkwill, started a new job in Khartoum, the capital of Sudan in North Africa.

In January Macmillan gave a speech in Ghana. Situated on the west coast of the vast continent of Africa, Ghana had been known as the Gold Coast whilst under British rule. Just three years earlier, in March 1957, the country had gained its independence under a well-known and charismatic leader named Kwame Nkrumah. A portly gentleman, who could hold an audience spellbound with decisive gestures and dramatic meaningful facial expressions, Nkrumah was feted for having fought for and won his country's early independence. He was seen by masses of Africans, as well as Black communities throughout the world, as not only the prime minister and leader of Ghana, but of Africa and of all downtrodden people.

Macmillan had chosen a particularly atmospheric location in which to deliver his speech, during which he famously stated: "The wind of change is blowing through this continent. Whether we like it or not, this growth of national consciousness is a political fact."

This speech then came to be significant as being the final signal for the end of colonial rule throughout Africa. Macmillan revised his famous speech and delivered it again a month later at the other end of the continent in Cape Town, South Africa.

The former British Anglo-Egyptian Sudan had already gained independence on 1st January 1956; the first in Africa to do so. An enormous country of expanses of wild territory, it comprised a fragile combination of two types of peoples: the Arab-Muslims in the north and the black Christians and Animists of the south. Antagonism between the two populations was long established, based on the northern Arabs having persistently through history invaded the south, capturing its inhabitants and selling them into slavery.

Having been drawn to North Africa as a national serviceman in Egypt some 15 years earlier, returning to work in aerial crop spraying in southern Sudan for a time, Peter had developed an affinity for this wild, beautiful and evolving region.

Seizing the opportunity to have the wind of change blow in his favour, Peter saw that, with colony after colony suddenly becoming independent of their colonial master, there was an urgent need for qualified professionals to train staff and organise the handover of key institutions to the people of the emerging new countries.

With his qualifications and experience as an aircraft fitter, Peter found himself a role training local ground staff of the national airline of Sudan, Sudan Airways, at Khartoum airport. Now married to Joan, he set up home in the city, staying until the contracts of all expatriate staff were terminated six years later. From Sudan he moved across the Red Sea to Aden in South Yemen, where he helped set up and run a new air force for that country as it headed for, and then achieved, its independence in 1967.

During the 1960s Peter and Joan, and within a short time, my younger brother and I in tow, found themselves living the last vestiges of an exciting and privileged lifestyle in a colonial bubble within a fast-changing post-colonial world.

This chapter is dedicated to the very unusual time of what I call "the last heydays" of colonialism of both Sudan and Aden. This was a time, in my opinion, before reality kicked in, the expatriates having to return to the normality of their native homelands, the newly formed countries being left to finally go it alone.

Last Heydays: Sudan

1960 was a turning point year for both Peter and Joan. After four years of marriage, he was tiring of traipsing around the airfields of the UK chasing work. Contracts were brief, the weather inclement, especially compared to what he had known during national service in Egypt and cotton spraying in Sudan. He was finding it impossible to save money to buy a home for himself and his new wife. To date they had lived in lodgings above a radio shop near Bournemouth, then in a caravan, which they towed from site to site as they moved around the country.

Joan meanwhile, having agreed with a wish of his, on their engagement, not to have children, was becoming broody. What had begun after a couple of years of marriage as a murmur of her subtle hints was now reaching a crescendo of bold entreaties to start a family together. Peter hit on a plan, a pact, if you like. Joan could have a baby if she would agree to live in Sudan. She did agree, he found a job and a place to live in Sudan's capital, Khartoum, and very soon they were there.

I have been lucky enough with this part of the chapter to have obtained a second memoir from Ted Weinel who wrote in the previous chapter about crop spraying in Sudan. Here he shares his memories of my dad from Khartoum days. Ted knew Dad and the world that he lived in then far better than I could have as a young child.

Ted's account follows:
Peter Balkwill became one of my new friends in July 1961. It was through the circumstances of my recently found employment with a company specialising in aerial crop spraying in the Sudan, which brought about the acquaintance.

After a short period at my new employer's headquarter base on the Isle of Wight, I was sent to the Sudan. The day after our own arrival in the Sudan, my colleague, Trevor, and I set about preparing for the arrival of the crop spraying aircraft after the long ferry flight that transported them from UK.

The preparations included designating four parking slots for the aircraft on the edge of Khartoum airport's large apron, south of the then terminal building. As it happened, that area was almost immediately in front of the Sudan Airways maintenance hangar. Being that time of the year, just before the spraying season began in the cotton fields, there were already a number of light, spraying aircraft lined up on the pan in readiness for the coming spray season. Having marked our slots, Trevor suggested we pay a visit to the airways' ground support equipment workshops, to say hello to a friend with whom he had worked in crop spraying back in previous years when DH Tiger Moth aircraft and small Bell 47 helicopters had been used for spraying.

Peter Balkwill invited us into his air-conditioned office for a welcome glass of ice-cold lemonade. It was mid-morning and the tropical heat on the airport's aprons was extreme, especially for newly arrived people from the temperate climate of a British summer. Peter was very pleased

to meet up with Trevor again since the last spray season and welcomed me into his fraternity of aviation associates with kindly hospitality. He was from Devonshire and since I was fresh from the West Country myself, there seemed to be a natural affinity between us.

Abdel Baqi Mohamed,
General Manager, Sudan Airways
Requests the pleasure of the company of
MR. & MRS. P. BRKWILL
for a reception party at his residence No. 5 Gamhouria Avenue on 30th July, 1964 to bid farewell to Captain D.W. Graham on the occasion of his final retirement.
From 07.30 to 09.00 p.m.

R.S.V.P. 72124

Invitation to Peter and Joan to a Sudan Airways party. Peter had joined the airline, in charge of the ground support workshops, and was training local staff in Khartoum, in 1960.

The common denominator was aviation, of course. Both Trevor and Peter were ex-national servicemen who had continued in aviation after demobilisation, as civilian aircraft engineers. I was purely civilian and barely out of my long engineering apprenticeship. This didn't matter however, since aviation and specifically aerial crop spraying was the profession with which we were all involved.

It was a short visit, but conversation eventually led to an invitation to visit with Peter to dine and to meet his wife, Joan, in their company house on the edge of the city, one evening during the following days, as a sort of welcome back celebration. In those times, the Sudan was emerging from the transition into independence. Khartoum was a multinational population and socially, religiously and politically liberal. Many European communities were in evidence, lending their skills in commerce, engineering and agriculture, and medicine to a developing nation. The winds of change were sweeping through much of Africa but some of the colonial habits remained in the form of social clubs dedicated to particular European groups.

On the town: Peter, 3rd from front on left, and Joan, front right, have fun with friends, drawn from a range of Khartoum's international communities.

Such was the Sudan Club, a place where British passport holders and their families might find relaxation in gentle surroundings, away from the bustling city life. The club provided for sporting activities such as tennis and swimming, the facilities of a lending library, a snooker room, two bars and a rather Victorian dining room. The club house with broad verandas sat at the centre of lawns and gardens, which in turn were encompassed by a high wall and ancient trees. The establishment was close to the banks of the Blue Nile, not far from the Grand Hotel with its landing stages for Nile paddle steamers. The Grand was probably the oldest of the few hotels in the city.

The entire British expat community of Khartoum gathered for a garden party to honour the Queen's visit in 1965. Although they cannot be seen in this official photo, Peter and Joan were there. The Queen can just be seen at the centre of the crowd.

Trevor and I shared a room at one of the other two, newer, Greek owned hotels in the city centre, the Metropole Hotel, or simply the Metro. Our company favoured the Metro because it was convenient, the company's Sudanese subsidiary offices being in the building next door. The other hotel was close by on the corner of an intersection and called the Acropolis. Both hotels catered to capacity for the influx of crop spraying people on their annual contractual visits.

Prior to joining the national airline, Sudan Airways, Peter Balkwill had worked at various locations with companies involved in crop spraying work, including the UK, Egypt and the Sudan. As mentioned, such work was seasonal and it was perfectly normal for the contract managers, pilots and engineering staff to "live rough" on location. Not many contracting companies were permanently established at that time and so the work did not carry married/accompanied positions. Clearly, after Peter was married he had looked for other employment, preferably overseas because of the better pay, etc., where he might be accompanied by his wife and family. There had been a suitable opening at Sudan Airways providing such an arrangement, so Peter became a member of that company's married/accompanied engineering staff.

However, as a result of his previous experiences with crop spraying, Peter was eager to maintain contact with the people and the life he had shared on those various, spray seasons over the years, hence his continuing friendship with Trevor, and then with me also, a "green" newcomer to the business. A couple of evenings later Peter picked us up in his little Fiat 500 and drove Trevor and me to his company house on the urbanised outskirts of the city. There were many similar houses dedicated to European living, each having its own garden and domestic staff accommodation attached. It was the custom of earlier times for European residences to employ domestic services, usually in the form of a houseboy who would assist with the daily household chores. Richer families of Victorian and early 20th century tropical living would employ cooks and nannies, also. However, in 1961 most foreign families living and working in the Sudan would have just a houseboy. This style of living would apply to single or unaccompanied men, too. The exception would be when several or many unaccompanied European men were employed and who worked together. In this case they would have a staff of stewards, houseboys, laundry boys, cooks and gardeners to look after a complete colony of living quarters in the form of a "mess", as in the armed forces.

Peter, on left, and friends (second left is Trevor, mentioned by Ted in this chapter) relax in the back garden of our Khartoum villa. Dated 1962.

Peter's wife Joan greeted us with great commotion, welcoming us into her household; seemingly very pleased to have visitors to dine. She had decided that we would eat outside in the garden where it was cooler than indoors. It was a jolly evening in which the beers and the meal were served by Joan and the houseboy. It was certainly an evening to remember, especially since the hotel food had begun to be a boring repetition even after only a week.

Joan was pregnant and looked forward to making a trip to the UK for the birth of their first child (Helen). Both she and Peter were excited at the prospect. Their trip would likely occur whilst Trevor and I were down country for the spray season. Of course, they had many friends in the crop spraying world and Joan insisted in calling all of them her "Bush Babies". They were always made very welcome in the Balkwill household.

– Ted Weinel, Denia, 30th July 2017

From a rented apartment and caravan sites to living in a house with grounds, attended by a servant, amid a social whirl that even included hobnobbing with the Queen, Peter certainly made the most of the last colonial heydays of Sudan.

The air carrier for British Aden, the flight crew of Aden Airways was almost exclusively British.

Last Heydays: Aden

Movement within the Arab world is fluid, almost as if it is a legacy of the nomadic tradition. So, it seems, colonial expatriates in the Middle East were also given to travelling freely about the region. My family did its fair share of foreign travel from Khartoum; Kenya, Egypt and up to Athens and Rome in southern Europe. Peter did work for the airline after all. However, we never went to Aden at that time, despite the air route from Khartoum to Aden being a well-flown one, so Alan, Peter's colleague at Sudan Airways, told me. Compared to reasonably sedate Sudan, Aden was at that time a melting pot city that was full of fun; clubs, bars, restaurants and cinemas. Acts of all nationalities coming to entertain at such venues as the Rock Hotel at Steamer Point. The plate glass windows of its panoramic roof top bar looked onto the shimmering waters of the harbour on the one side, and the barren rocks of Aden on the other; multi-coloured lights, set into its ceiling, pulsating over the dance floor all night, long before discotheques became fashionable.

This is Steamer Point. The Rock Hotel, with its terracotta-coloured wrap around balconies, rises up in the background. Its roof top bar had panoramic views and coloured lights in the ceiling.

It was also a duty-free port with one of the busiest harbours in the world at that time, fully stocked with international bargains; jewellery and pearls from the Gulf, electronics, cameras, watches, fine china and toys from Japan, and chic perfumes from Europe. One Indian-owned store, named Bhicagee Cowasjee, situated in Tawahi, a short walk from where the liners disgorged the bargain-hungry passengers that were making Aden boom at Steamer Point, famously stocked it all. Aden expatriates would be sure to avoid these crowds, and the inflated prices they allegedly caused, choosing to buy at Bhicagee Cowasjee on the days the fewest liners were in port. And many can still remember entering that Aladdin's cave of attractive goods for sale on display. I have heard them talk of having bought things from there as diverse as a single golf club, records (apparently this was where the resident forces radio DJs selected the music for their shows each week), a sewing machine, a cine camera, a dinner service and so on. Meanwhile, in the back alleys of Tawahi, a tailor could knock up a bespoke outfit from quality material almost while the customer waited. So, Aden was a magnet holiday destination for Khartoum expatriates, where they could also buy cheap yet luxury merchandise.

Peter was, of course, to end up going to Aden to work in the traumatic year of independence (1967), and the fallout from it, of 1968–1969. But this is an account of the last colonial heydays of Aden that led up to that time.

As I have no personal connection with this period in Aden that I am writing about, I have turned to others who have shared with me their memories of it.

Jenny arrived in Aden as a young adult to join her parents. A generation ahead of my dad (1953–1957), her father had worked as an engineer for Sudan Airways in Khartoum. Then he had transferred, contracted by the British airline BOAC, to Aden Airways in Aden. He was to remain with the airline until the end in 1967.

There he lived comfortably with his wife in a smart block of six apartments named Atlanta House in Dolphin Square (as already mentioned many places in British Aden were named for London and British locations and landmarks, such as Dolphin Square, which is in Pimlico, London) at the Steamer Point end of the Ma'alla Straight. They had a Somali *ayah* to look after them.

Life was good and Jenny was thrilled to join them, beginning work as an air stewardess with Aden Airways in 1961. She remained with the airline until leaving Aden in 1964.

Jenny's period in Aden encompassed only the stirrings of what would become the vicious fight for independence that marked the following years up to the 1967 British withdrawal. She says she felt absolutely safe there. Transport was sent to fetch her for the airport at Khormaksar, and she loved her job flying with Aden Airways around the Middle East. Just a few of the routes into dangerous parts of the South Yemen interior were not available to her as a member of female staff.

In fact, Jenny says, those three and a half years in British Aden were some of the best of her life. She says she did not spend a night at home in that period. There was so much to do and so many diverse, fun and interesting people to be with.

A typical day would start at Tarshayn Beach, nowadays known as Sahel al-Aroosa, a Yemeni resort. It was a dedicated officers' beach, and that is where everyone went to meet and agree their social diary for the day. The company there was predominately male and young, so single ladies such as Jenny were in high demand and there was always an invitation for them.

There were VIP invites to cocktail receptions and the beating of the retreat on the aircraft carriers of Navy friends, parties in private houses, the open-air cinema at Khormaksar, dinners in restaurants, at the airport restaurant, curry at Holkat Bay, Chinese in Ma'alla perhaps, or even a beach barbecue.

The Kuwait crisis of that era was raging, so many personnel from all three of the armed forces were moving through Aden between the UK and the Gulf. According to Jenny it was a case of a huge circle of people revolving in a small space, all of whom were socialising almost all of the time. For leisure Jenny would horse ride on the beach at Khormaksar, swim, water-ski and, when the tide would be up at monsoon season, surf at Tarshayn. She learnt to glide at Sheikh Othman. There were picnic trips upcountry, courtesy of RAF aircraft and boat rides to the Blue Grotto cave off shore in an RAF launch.

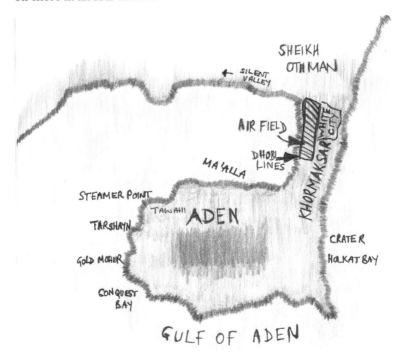

Appropriately named Conquest Bay because it was unreachable by road due to surrounding walls of rocks on three sides and the sea to the other, parties of young people were known to spend a day climbing the rocks to picnic and swim there. Not only relishing the challenge of the rock climb, they would also brave the sea there, as there was no shark net at Conquest Bay.

Not everyone in Aden was attached to the forces. Jenny remembers civilian friends also, working in international trading companies or for shipping agents. There were also foreign company owners; Indian, Greek, Lebanese, for example. But she does not remember having any Adeni/Yemeni acquaintances.

Then there was her parents' age group. Jenny remembers that the older generation would gather for dinner parties, and to play Mahjong. As her father was an employee of Aden Airways, her parents qualified for membership of the civilian-only Gold Mohur beach club, where there was a shark net so safe swimming and diving were possible. There was also a fine bar and restaurant.

Bottled in Aden, Stim — a brand of fizzy drink that was very refreshing in the searing Aden heat — was beloved by expats and Adenis alike.

Sheila, like Jenny, an Aden Airways stewardess, had also followed her parents to Aden in 1961. They had previously lived in Free Town, Sierra Leone, where her father had worked in public works for the Crown Agents leading up to that country's independence. Sheila flew at that time with Sierra Leone Airways.

Once in Aden, Sheila got her Aden Airways job after a chance meeting with the airline's personnel officer at Gold Mohur club. She stayed with them up until the withdrawal in 1967, by which time she had become Chief Stewardess. Sheila told me that the only female personnel allowed to stay until the end were air stewardesses and nurses because of the vital work they were carrying out. In the case of the stewardesses, they were staffing the flights that were evacuating the various different nationalities out of Aden back to their home countries.

Like Jenny, Sheila remembers a happy time in Aden. Where Jenny left in 1964, Sheila remained through the difficult years to the end, but still did not personally experience any trouble, although she would learn of problems, usually by word of mouth rather than any other medium as she did not have a television or a radio. These included the lobbing of grenades from vantage points onto patrols of soldiers in Land Rovers, and the re-taking of Crater by the Argylls under the leadership of their infamous leader Colonel "Mad Mitch" Mitchell. Sheila and the other stewardesses lived in flats at Khormaksar that had netting rigged around their verandahs to repel grenades, but none were ever thrown there.

Sheila was a keen horsewoman, riding horses belonging to Sheikhs in weekend races at a Khormaksar polo field, where the other jockeys were Arab men and British Army officers. Often they rode stallions that had not been broken in. As Jenny did, Sheila would ride at Khormaksar Beach in the mornings. As a longer exercise she would also ride out of Aden, eastwards along the coast, towards Hadhramaut.

There they might at times be greeted by villagers firing guns in welcome which of course frightened the horses, and Sheila had to ask them to refrain.

Sheila remembers working on scheduled flights upcountry, but no incidents of trouble there. In fact, her most vivid memory is of rural children being fascinated by the black court shoes that she wore as part of her airline uniform. She also remembers the aircraft cargo being unloaded onto camels and donkeys.

Back at the airport in Khormaksar, Sheila had a colleague and friend who was an NLF (National Liberation Front) member. He told her that his grievance against the British was not personal. He just wanted his country back "sooner rather than later".

Sheila married in Aden during the final days of the colony, and honeymooned in Nairobi. The plane which had transported her there was blown up by a bomb on the airstrip at Khormaksar following its return trip. That was the closest she came to trouble in Aden at the end of a carefree time there.

Boy from the Moor

Chapter Ten

Family Life in Sudan

1962. In the garden of the
Khartoum villa, Mum and I.

Boy from the Moor, the story about Peter Balkwill, has reached the top of its arc. Previous chapters have traced my dad's ambitions and achievements from childhood up to attaining the job and lifestyle in Sudan that he desired. But from hereon in, the story unfolds progressively downwards to his untimely end, by way of the problems inherent with the post-colonial expat lifestyle he was living, and a world that was fast moving into a brand new era.

The story of this downward trajectory begins with an account of the challenges of family life in post-colonial, expat Sudan. Presented from the points of view of each of the characters of the Balkwill household, I will begin with my mum — Peter's wife Joan — who, arguably, faced the greatest struggle.

Joan's Story

Food shopping at the *souk* in Khartoum.

Arrival

Joan, aged 26 and pregnant with her first child, arrived for the first time in Khartoum to a comfortable, furnished villa with landscaped gardens to front and back. It was the home her husband, Peter, had dreamed of providing for them both. It was spacious, and there was not one but there were two kitchens, a very large living and dining area, as well as outdoor sitting and eating facilities on the extensive verandahs that surrounded the house. There were two enormous bedrooms with a third, al fresco, sleeping area on the flat roof of the property, and two things which perhaps surprisingly, she had not grown up with in the UK: a bathroom and indoor (honey bucket) toilet.

Something else that came with the Khartoum house that she had not before known was a servant, or houseboy, or *sufragi*, depending on whom you talked to. Indeed, Joan came from a family with a history of being in service themselves. She had grown up in a tied cottage on an estate where relatives had been employed by the landed family of her village. Lawaya, Joan's Khartoum servant, lived in quarters in the villa's back garden.

Peter, who already knew Khartoum and Sudan well, had arrived in the country ahead of her. He had been solely responsible for choosing their old, probably Edwardian, British colonial bungalow. It was situated behind high walls and an enormous pair of heavy wooden gates in Mogran, in the southern Khartoum suburbs. It was sandwiched between Khartoum University to the front and a zoo behind. The reason for this choice of location, his colleague Alan, from Sudan Airways, told me, was that it was on the road from the city towards the cotton fields of Al Gezira in the south, where he had worked prior to his marriage, and where his greatest friends were still employed as crop sprayers, and living quite rough. Peter and Joan were to make their Khartoum home a haven for these men during their recreational visits to the capital. Most other Khartoum expatriates lived together in modern accommodation purpose built for them, in the "New Quarter" of the city, some distance from Mogran. Peter had sacrificed the opportunity of an orderly life amongst fellow Europeans for them both for an existence that was raw, on the edge, and by turns, exciting and stressful.

The Khartoum villa was spacious and comfortable. This photo is of the front entrance, which was shaded by the large covered verandah. To the left is one of the property's two kitchens. To the right (not shown here) were the indoor sleeping quarters, stairs to the rooftop sleeping area (located above the entrance), and the bathroom and toilet. The spacious living area occupied the entire middle of the house and there was an extensive, covered verandah to the rear, which housed further sitting and eating areas.

Joan had been abroad only once in her life before Khartoum, and this had been a short visit to an uncle and aunt in Germany, who were stationed there after the war. She had certainly never been anywhere as hot, dusty, far away and different as Khartoum. She often told me that she had been initially overwhelmed by her new life in Sudan.

What to do with such a large house? She struggled to come to terms with the idea that rather than do the housework and gardening herself, as her peers were doing back home in the UK, she was to direct Lawaya to carry out the domestic work and a team of gardeners to tend the ample grounds. But it was clear that she would need the help. Keen, though, to at least set up her new "nest" to her own standards, she told me that, on arrival, she set rebelliously about cleaning the kitchen herself, much to the consternation of Peter, who wished for her to settle quickly into the role of mistress of the colonial household, and nervously eyed by Lawaya who worried she would put him out of a job.

Joan scrubbed the walls so vehemently on that occasion that she dislodged a shard of flaking paint, spearing the delicate flesh beneath her finger nail and causing septicaemia that laid her low for days. On another occasion, when she came across Lawaya washing his feet in a bowl in the second kitchen, she lost her temper. To her, this practice carried out in a kitchen was unhygienic, whereas his point of view was that he was making himself clean in order to enter the main kitchen and the house. This was to be just the first of the culture clashes between the pair, and a major challenge for Joan. But happily, they went on to form a bond, and he was to help her to come to terms with her new role. Regarding the two kitchens, he showed her that the second kitchen was where he was to carry out heavy work such as food preparation and pot washing, and the main kitchen was to be her domain to cook meals for her family and guests. An arrangement that Joan was to be happy with over the course of her six years in Khartoum.

And it was Lawaya who was to act as interpreter for Joan and guide her in her daily transactions with local people whilst Peter, who was a fluent Arabic speaker, was away at work. He explained local customs to her, and accompanied her into the streets of Khartoum. At the *souk* he would haggle on her behalf for the meat and vegetables she required. A remarkable, yet positive aspect at that time, she told me years later, was how abundant and fresh the produce, that had been brought in from the fertile shores of the Nile, was in Khartoum. She had grown up in the UK during World War II and during its aftermath, on a diet of rationing and substitute food. Lawaya introduced Joan to foods she had never before seen, and showed her how to prepare and eat them, for example okra, aubergine, *ta'miyas* (a kind of falafel) and the limes which he would transform daily into gloriously refreshing *laymoon* (limeade).

Social Life

Luckily for Joan, the alien way of life in Khartoum that at first daunted her was to be eased by the man that she had at first mistrusted but who would become her ally. But Lawaya could not help where Joan's expat social life was concerned. Her first and foremost problem revolved around the old fashioned, peculiarly British, institution of class. In Khartoum, she often told me, life was lived to a particular type of expat hierarchy. What job you did, your background in the UK, your credentials as a colonial, it all mattered, apparently. And amongst the wives as much, if not more, than with the husbands. For Joan this presented a special kind of hell as, coming from a working class and humble background, she simply had no coping mechanism for dealing with this. Indeed, she had never before faced such a phenomenon. Worse still, events would revolve mostly around the grand institutions of the British Empire; the Sudan Club, the Cathedral and grounds, the Nile Sailing Club, The Grand Hotel and so on, where a certain level, unfathomable to her, of decorum and manners were expected. Peter was not much help as he found such socialising naturally easy to do and apparently had little empathy for her in this respect. According to her, he would simply tell her "have faith in yourself" and "don't follow the sheep". However close friends of his were more understanding and obliging and she received guidance from them that would sustain her through her Khartoum experience, in particular from Peter's friends Alan and Sue.

Then there were the Sudanese friends and expats of differing ethnic groups. Peter had many friends amongst the various nationality groups of Khartoum, whom Joan was expected to mix with in social settings, and to entertain at home.

Although it took a little time to get to know their different ways, Joan found it easier to get on with Peter's various non-British friends than with the Brits. She instinctively warmed to them as fellow foreigners in Khartoum. In particular she felt an affinity with the Greek community. These people were generally business owners who had been present in Sudan since the turn of the century. Belonging to one of the countries of non-colonial powers in Africa, they had been encouraged, apparently, by the British ruling authorities at that time, to come to the country to oil its commercial wheels. They could be found living and thriving through-out the country, right down to Juba near the southern border with Uganda. Peter and Joan would socialise with them in the hotels of Khartoum and at the international cabaret, and they would visit each other's homes.

Peter and Joan became close to one Greek family in particular. Stelios Panera, who insisted on anglicising his name to Steve in order to blend in with his British friends, owned a successful foundry in the city. He was well off and he and his family lived travelling between comfortable homes in Khartoum and Athens, both of which Peter and Joan and family visited regularly during their six Khartoum years. His wife, Evridiki, was very helpful to Joan, and for a long while the impressionable Joan became immersed in Greek culture, courtesy of her. It was during this period that she gave birth to both of us children, giving us Greek-based names: Helen and Peter. For years afterwards, Joan would refer to us using the Greek nicknames that Evridiki had called us as babies: Elenita and Petros. This was long after the days of Khartoum. We were now living regular lives back in the UK and our dad, Peter senior, was dead. The Paneras were by now a distant memory to Joan, and almost unknown to us kids, to whom the nicknames, given to us during another era, were an ongoing source of confusion.

Mum, Dad and I pose with Evridiki Panera and her daughter, probably in Athens rather than in Khartoum.

But then, ten years after leaving Khartoum, and following the trauma of losing Peter in Aden and having to return to the UK to take care of her children alone, Joan was to receive a sad shock when she was persuaded to take the kids to visit the Paneras in Athens.

In the mid-1960s, along with dismissing the Europeans that were assisting the local workforce of the new, post-colonial Sudan, the authorities had also nationalised the assets of the Greek community, driving them to leave also.

And so, Joan arrived to find the Paneras living in a crowded flat in a dusty street in Athens. Where once she used to stay with them in an elegant apartment in the city's fashionable seaside suburb of Glyfada, now she saw them subjected to austerity. Where she had once known Steve as the owner of his own successful company, in his advancing years, he was now working as a welder at the docks in the port of Piraeus. I was there and witnessed a joyful yet sorrowful reunion between them all.

Steve was excited and proud to have us visit him and went on to take us on a tour of his country, including his native island. Agios Efstratios is a little speck of land in the northern Aegean Sea, and, at the time, was exclusively Greek and quite closed to the outside world. We arrived in rowboats from the Athens ferry. Whilst on Efstratios, I learned that the island had lost many of its inhabitants to emigration to North Africa, much of it within the living memories of some remaining inhabitants. I met one old woman who was still consumed with bitterness that much of her family had left without her when she was a young woman. They had gone on to have prosperous expat lives where she had been left living a frugal and rural life up to that present day.

It seems that the impact of empire on ordinary folk and their families who had chosen to live at least part of their lives within it affected people of all nationalities.

Back in the UK in 1967 we pose for a photo to be sent out to Dad, who was still working abroad. Following her comfortable life in Sudan my mum found running a household alone and without help very difficult.

127

Wife and Motherhood

There is no doubt that Joan, despite its challenges, enjoyed Khartoum life. Indeed, in summing up, as she was approaching the end of her reasonably long life, she told me that it had been her best era. But I don't think that it, and marriage to my father, the *Boy from the Moor*, turned out to be quite what she had expected or hoped for.

Clearly Peter had a strong personal remit in Sudan, and Joan, still impressionable and quite biddable at eight years younger than him, was caught up in his slipstream. Whilst I feel that he did love her, I do however also think that he understood and exploited her vulnerability, if only to progress his own enthusiasms.

And so, Joan was required to walk a fine line between various roles in Khartoum: doting and seductive wife, new mother, mistress of her household, hostess and socialite. And on some occasions, unexpected challenges she faced with him could be frightening. For instance the party that Peter took her to at an apartment kept for crew of a foreign airline, where dancing was interrupted by a shoot-out in the street, a stray bullet entering the room via an open window, ricocheting off the walls above the bodies of prostrate party goers who had thrown themselves to the floor, before exhausting itself and dropping down.

It must have been exhausting, not least where balancing being a wife and a mother were concerned.

Joan became a new mother very quickly after arriving for the first time in Khartoum. After a short time there she returned for several weeks to her hometown in the UK in order to give birth. She was able, therefore, to receive important advice and encouragement from her parents during that crucial time of early motherhood.

Back in Khartoum however, having undertaken the return transcontinental flight on her own with her six-week-old baby, she quickly came to miss the guidance of her family.

She told me that, back in Sudan with her baby, she soon began to feel very alone. She became what she called "blue". She told her friend Sue about this, who, as a qualified nurse, then called a doctor. Mum says the doctor gave her a pill and then she felt better again. I assume that back in that day my mother had no idea about the condition of postnatal depression, or about antidepressants. Family of mine whose parents were recent immigrants to an underdeveloped part of Australia when their children were born, and therefore a long way from the support of family infrastructure in the UK, reported emotions and behaviour their mother displayed to be very similar to what Joan experienced as a young mother in Khartoum.

And just because they had a family now, Peter signalled that he had no intention of changing his life. My mother opened up about this late in her life, but it is also how I remember it as a child. Making sure that I was always safe, either at home with Lawaya, or on sleepovers in the home of friends, Alan and Sue, he insisted that his and Joan's hectic social life should continue. After all, he was the one that had never wanted children. She never ever said it, but I know that Mum eternally regretted that this caused a lifelong emotional distance between herself and me.

Also, Peter expected her to open up her home to guests she neither knew nor understood. Coffee on the front lawn in the morning, perhaps. Afternoon tea at the back, on the shady verandah when the strong African sun was still up, or out on the lawn if it was late afternoon approaching dusk, followed, at times, by a game of badminton on the full-size court that occupied the part of the lawn behind the house. Or maybe a big dinner party, with Lawaya in attendance, indoors amid the fading grandeur of the plush furnishings that the villa came equipped with. Generous sofas and armchairs and elegant side tables, oriental rugs scattered on highly polished tile floors, voluminous curtains at the French doors and heavily framed copies of old masterpieces lining the thick distempered walls. Joan always remembered a cultured guest named Andy, who was a frequent visitor. He had taken her on a tour of the pictures in her house, explaining the scenes and naming their artists. She particularly remembered the scene of Paris, painted by Utrillo, which hung between two sets of French doors. Andy was a British Embassy friend of Peter's. Joan never knew how the pair had initially met. He also visited us once whilst we were in the UK, staying at the home of my maternal grandparents. But one day, whilst we were still living in Khartoum, Andy disappeared and we never heard of him again.

Even trying to decide whereabouts on the property to entertain could be a challenge for Joan. Within the house, Lawaya might be cleaning. Intensive and laborious work could be going on in any part of the gardens at any time. Khartoum lies on the fringes of the Sahara Desert, yet the villa's manmade gardens were particularly lush, with manicured lawns which required a lot of maintenance and watering. I remember that the gardening equipment was crudely made from wood, and that the gardening team would arrive with it piled on donkeys. If morning coffee on the front lawn was mistimed, then Joan risked her guests being treated to the overwhelming experience of noise, chaotic clamour and horrible stench of the regular arrival of the municipal honey bucket cart, come to our front gate to collect the contents of our toilet. Situated to the side of the property, the house's toilet fronted onto an internal courtyard, with its rear being one of the external walls of the house. Behind the toilet pan was a hole in the rear wall through which it could be retrieved to be emptied onto the honey bucket cart. Like the gardening equipment, the cart was fashioned from wood, and it was pulled by a donkey. My abiding fear as a young child in Khartoum was that, sitting on the toilet one day, I might get dragged through the hole, never to be seen again. I would have nightmares about it.

But probably the biggest stress for Joan about expat life was actually not when she was abroad, but the occasions she had to stay home alone in the UK with the children while Peter was out there working. This happened a few times, most notably throughout the year of 1967, when he completed the Sudan contract and moved across to begin in Aden, in advance of us joining him in 1968.

Aside from missing the love and support of her partner, Joan, by all accounts, felt disorientated in the UK. No help in the house or garden. No help with the children. Unfamiliar systems and no structure to her day. And then there was the cold weather to contend with.

Expat life. Joan found it difficult both to live with it, and without it.

Lawaya's Story

A big part of Lawaya's daily routine was to look after me, from my babyhood until we left Khartoum when I was five.

Lawaya's full name was Lawaya Abdullah Paypay. He hailed from the southern Sudanese city of Juba. This was at a time before the autonomous country of South Sudan came into being, and when the entire Sudan was the largest country in Africa. Lawaya, in common with the majority of fellow southerners, a Christian, had travelled a long way from home to find work in Muslim dominated Khartoum.

As far as we know Lawaya enjoyed his job. He would smile a lot. Although I was a young child at the time, I remember him as caring and gentle. Looking after me was to him, I think, a major part of holding down what he considered to be his good job. I would while away hours with him as he performed his chores around the house. He had endless patience with me, praising me as I performed childhood feats before him such as running and skipping and singing. He taught me Arabic words, and he helped me out of a whole host of scrapes that I got myself into. For example, him climbing in through a ceiling height window to retrieve me from the bathroom that I, at aged only four years old, had locked myself into is just one such occasion that I clearly remember.

A humorous aside, from an observation made by my mother, arising from his view of children according to the culture he came from, were the two varying remarks he made on both arrivals back in Sudan from the UK by her with each of her new born babies. On the occasion she introduced him to her first born, i.e. me, a female child, he reportedly uttered *Malesh*, which is Arabic for "never mind". Whereas, when he met my baby brother for the first time, a boy, he exclaimed *alhamdulillah* meaning "praise be to God". Anyway, no matter my status as the inferior child, I remember fondly how well Lawaya looked after me, and feel lucky to have had his influence on my early life.

I know that my father rated Lawaya highly, and the two men respected each other. They would speak Arabic together. By all accounts Lawaya was very upset when the Balkwill family left Khartoum, although relieved that Peter had found him a good replacement job with his Rhodesian friend, Ted Bell, who was going to be staying on in Sudan.

In 1969, just months before Peter was killed, Lawaya sent him, via Ted Bell, the letter shown on the following pages. He expresses fond wishes to Peter and his family. And he asks Peter for a "hand o' clock", which is a wristwatch. By all accounts Peter did send him the watch, which made him very happy.

Lawaya stands by his *tukal* at the bottom of the Khartoum villa's garden.

LAWAYA PAY PAY
c/o. MR. H. E. BELL
P.O. BOX 2619
KHARTOUM — SUDAN.

23rd. February 1969

Dear P.O. Baykwill,

Thank you very much for
your letter received by me

All of us quite here we hope
That this letter will find you in

Good kondition all of you especially
The childonm and Their mother too

Mr. P.O. I hope in future you
will send me as a Prize "HAND 6clock"
with KALANDER and many Thanks for

But Mr. Bell leaving Sudan for good
at the month of APRIL — you will Send me the
Oclock at an early date

134

My Best wishes and warmest
from Sudan to all of you

Thanking you in anticipation

Yours Sincerely.

LAWAYA PATAY

SUDAN.

In 1964 Lawaya had to flee Khartoum for safety. According to my mother he took a crowded train, perching on its roof, back to his home city in the deep south. That would have meant hours and hours of precariously clinging on, whilst exposed to the elements. To have remained in the city, particularly as the Balkwill villa was situated at the heart of the turmoil that was going on at Khartoum University opposite the house, would have been for him, a southerner, very dangerous. Tensions that had begun building up at independence between Sudan's Muslim north and Christian south had exploded.

At independence in 1956, the British had left behind a pretty strong civilian government. However, any of the good things about the new country only benefitted its northern part. As it had been during colonial rule, the south was mostly neglected and left out of governance. The vast majority of government posts during independence had been given to northerners. Following independence, the realities of politics dawned on Sudan's leaders. Abdullah Khalil, the first Prime Minister, suffered severe problems both at home and abroad. Then in 1958 he quietly stepped aside, allowing the top general of the military, Ibrahim Abboud, to take over the country. Whilst Abboud was successful with the economy and bringing stability, his treatment of the south was disastrous. He tried to enact a policy of imposing Islamic and Arabic culture on the majority Christian population there. Abboud then disbanded Parliament. The southern Sudanese protested and were met with forceful, heavy-handed measures. A rebellion that turned into full-scale civil war, fuelled by outside interests, followed.

In 1963 Abboud called for national discussion on problems in the south. This turned into platforms to speak out against his government as a whole. Massive student protests at Khartoum University followed. The government then responded by cracking down, ruining Abboud's popularity and support, even among the northern Sudanese. By 1964, Abboud had been forced out and Sudan was once again under civilian rule. It was during the 1964 election, when rioting took place at Khartoum University, opposite the Balkwill villa, that Lawaya had to escape.

During Lawaya's absence a friend of his, named Jumea, came to work temporarily for the Balkwills. Jumea was a Muslim and therefore immune to the threat facing Christians, such as Lawaya, in rebellious Khartoum at the time. But Peter and Joan found that Jumea was stealing from them. A selection of insignificant household items, such as soap and an airline holdall disappeared. I accompanied my dad when he went to the *tukal*, to dismiss Jumea. I was, at that point, seeing the inside of Lawaya's quarters for the first time and found it very surprising for its rudimentary living conditions compared to our own house across the lawn. The two men shouted a lot at each other in Arabic and gesticulated angrily. I had never seen anything quite like it before, especially from what I had always known as my easy-going father. And it was the first time I had ever heard the word "fired", as in immediately ending a person's employment. I thought of it as an aggressive word and the whole experience really rather frightened me.

Lawaya eventually returned to us, and calm, normality and the effective running of the household resumed.

Soon after Lawaya received the wristwatch Peter had sent him from Aden, via Ted Bell, in 1969, Ted had to tell him that Peter had died. Apparently Lawaya wept at the news. This was the last report Joan was ever to receive of her former servant and friend.

Helen's Story

At play in the grounds of the Khartoum villa.

My own memories of Sudan tend to come in extremes. Hours on end of solitary freedom within the grounds of the Khartoum villa, no supervision other than Lawaya's watchful eye at a distance. Yet also being regularly dressed up to the nines to attend a most enormous schedule of functions with the many other children of the Khartoum expat community, all of us wearing our party best. These kids came in all ages, both boys and girls, and I would be thrown in and expected to mix.

Probably Christmas 1965, a children's party at the Sudan Club.

My father was keen that I should lack no experience in my young life. I was therefore sent to school in Khartoum at such a young age that I don't even remember my first day there. Nor do I remember a time in my life when I could not read or write, since I started learning so young. I guess I would have been about three.

I do, however, remember my final year or so of school, before we left Khartoum for good when I was five. It was a small, privately owned, missionary-style school. We were taught in English, though the other pupils were a wide-ranging mix of nationalities, as well as Sudanese. I have the impression that not all children in Khartoum were sent to school as young as me. I was there because of my father's ambition for me. The owner and teacher was a Mrs Darbin — a long-time British expat.

Mrs Darbin's style of education was old fashioned but also encouraging and fair. It was therefore a strange and confusing experience when I attended a local infants school during a year back in the UK, after Sudan and before Aden, where I had to "learn" to read and write all over again and in a very different and modern system.

Oftentimes Dad would be the one to collect me from Mrs Darbin's at lunchtime and take me around as he went about his Khartoum business. There wasn't really anywhere I didn't go with him: in the tool sheds and on the planes at his work at the airport, to bars and to the Sudan Club, to the *souk* to snack on a fast lunch of my favourite treat, *ta'miyas* (chickpea falafel), followed by popcorn, both cooked freshly on braziers in front of us. There was always an amiable chuck under the chin or an adoring squeeze of my white-skinned cheek from the cheerful Sudanese vendors. We would also go to the businesses and shops of his Greek friends. In particular I liked to visit Menas at his dairy and bakery, where I would always receive a freshly whizzed banana milkshake. On one occasion, whilst parallel parking in the *souk*, outside Menas' shop, Dad's leg jerked (he was unaware at that time that he had a condition affecting the cartilage in his knee) and he ploughed into the stationary car in front of us. It was a very frightening moment indeed.

As a child in the garden with Lawaya, I enjoyed a very carefree childhood existence. With my parents, in particular my Dad, by contrast, I had a very grown-up experience. This could be, by turns, interesting and fun and confusing and, sometimes, frightening.

Dad liked to make sure he introduced me to music and film. He kept a small gramophone at the house and played me music from all around the world, as well as a lot of jazz. I particularly associate the Stan Getz and Astrid Gilberto version of the song "Girl from Ipanema" with the Khartoum house.

And he liked to take me to the local, outdoor, cinema. I enjoyed seeing the films on the big screen, but did not always understand what they were about. There was never an explanation. The time is legendary in my family when I piped up that I could not understand why Bugs Bunny was a "cartoon" when I also lived in "Khartoum", the word sounded exactly the same to me.

The Coliseum was an outdoor cinema. Dad liked to take me to the cinema and obviously deemed it important to note my attendance at this particular film.

Making sense of my enclosed existence at the house compared to the hustle and bustle around us that was Khartoum, and why I lived in Sudan at all if, as I was repeatedly told, my family home was actually a place 3,000-odd miles away in the UK, was a tricky business.

Often, I remember, I would clamber up on to a horizontal strut of the villa's heavy wooden front gate. There I would watch with fascination a hotch-potch of daily local life splayed out right below me. I liked to think that where I could see a mass of white-robed, white-turbaned, ebony-faced men (for some reason it seemed like there were always men, with no women about), they could not see me. When I inadvertently dropped a hand-kerchief one time onto the dusty ground of the other side of the gate therefore, I was mortified, and a little terrified, when an old man interrupted his trotting donkey, jumped down from the saddle, pulled the beast towards me and leant down and picked up my hanky. Reaching up to me with it, however, he grinned a most enormous and reassuring toothless grin that let me know that my childish spying was okay by him.

Once I asked my mother why I had seen Arab men lying asleep by the dusty roadside outside our gate. Apparently, these were pilgrims on the journey from the western countries of Islamic north Africa towards Port Sudan to the east of us, and on, across the Red Sea, to Saudi Arabia and Mecca, for the Hajj. That would have been one heck of an overall journey, hence the need for their kip, and quite the test of faith, I feel.

Of course, I could also hear the muezzin's call to prayer from the local mosque several times daily from within the confines of our garden. I knew very well that this was a tradition that did not affect my Western, Christian family, but always wondered at it and what its role was in the lives of the Sudanese that surrounded us in Khartoum. Similarly, at Ramadan, the noise of a gun set off to signal the end of fasting was also baffling. On those occasions it was noticeable that the atmosphere was almost pin drop quiet up to the gun's resounding report, erupting into loud chatter and clanging and clattering of pots and pans and crockery as Khartoum's Muslim families, that I could hear but not see, began to feast.

Regarding my family's own religious tradition, my parents would keep a turkey all year, tethered to an enormous tree to the side of the garden. Each successive turkey would be called the same name of Terence. I would help Lawaya daily with the scattering of feed for Terence. On one occasion I was told that I was allowed to accompany Lawaya on a journey with Terence. An old flat bed truck, crowded with local people, rattled up to the gate of our house and Lawaya clambered up and into it, the turkey and myself being passed up to him. He clutched Terence under his arm throughout the bumpy journey to our destination. My memory is hazy about what happened next, but I know we returned without Terence. Some days later, as my parents, various invited guests and I tucked into a splendid Christmas lunch, there was much merriment as the adults discussed how tasty Terence was. A watershed moment for me, and early lesson in the harsh reality of life, I cried for days afterwards. My unexplained journey with Lawaya and Terence had, of course, been the turkey's last, as it had been to an abattoir.

What with so many confusing things going on around me, combined with multiple visitors to the house and my solitary existence in the grounds and house, I developed a heightened sense of imagination. I would lie awake in bed at night, alone, either in my enormous darkened bedroom or on a rope-slung temporary bed on the house's flat roof, where we tended to sleep on the hottest nights, staring up at stars and the colourful lights of aircraft, in a whirl of wakeful dreams. And at times these vivid thoughts would scare me. I developed a pair of imaginary friends, Gagula and Bagula, who I then fell out with, upsetting myself no end. My parents and Lawaya became extremely concerned as the days passed and my trauma about Gagula and Bagula failed to subside. The problem was only resolved when my father informed me that he was going to take my former friends to work at the airport with him that day and put them on a plane to Cairo. We all lined up to say goodbye to imaginary Gagula and Bagula. When Dad arrived home that day he reassured me that the pair had indeed been dispatched on the Egypt-bound plane and I never feared either of them again, much to the household's relief. I remember to this day that crazy episode.

A very real phenomenon that was equally as eerie as my imaginations were the Saharan sand storms that whipped around us from time to time. Lawaya and my mother would collectively sense when one was approaching, as the atmosphere outside would become deathly still and silent. Then it would be a case of rushing around the house shuttering the windows, drawing curtains and rolling up rugs against the doors. The dump of desert sand on us as a result of these storms was all enveloping. And it was definitely best to prevent it from leaking into the house where it could seep into everything and be almost impossible to completely remove.

Comparing all of the facets of Sudan life to my home country of the UK that we returned to for ten weeks leave every year was intriguing and at times mystifying.

People in the UK were different to anyone I knew in Sudan, even British expatriates. They were used to ordinary, everyday life and therefore more down to earth than what I was accustomed to. We would divide our time between my two sets of grandparents and I lived their daily experiences with them; cooking, housework, tending the veg patch, catching the red double decker bus to town. In Devon I could not even understand many of my paternal relatives as their West Country accents were so thick. And then there was the temperature. I was really quite old, and cognisant, before I first ever felt cold. This actually occurred in Rome, on a layover during one annual UK-bound journey from Sudan. In the black of night, during a bus journey from the airport to a hotel, I began to cry. When I was asked what was wrong I couldn't describe it. As my distress escalated, so did the concern of the other passengers on the bus. Everybody was trying to find out what was wrong with me, according to my mother. Hungry? Tired? Thirsty? In pain? No, none of them. In the end someone worked out that I was actually cold, and that the acute distress that I felt at it was because I had never experienced such a sensation before. I had lived my entire life up to that point either in hot, hot Sudan or the UK in the summer time.

Illness and illness prevention, living between the two different environments, were a real issue. I had to have a number of inoculations regularly against diseases in Sudan, the effects of which would lay me low for days. I had to take malaria tablets at meal times and had to have extra salt added to my food due to loss of sodium through sweating in the Khartoum heat. Back in the UK I would always come down with at least one bout of tonsillitis or flu per visit. And I would regularly vomit for the first few days after arriving at either end, before re-acclimatising to the local food, water and conditions.

Living in expat, post-colonial Sudan was a strange way to grow up. And it certainly gave me a special set of childhood challenges, the effects of which have lived on with me into my adult life. And it presented my mother and father with parenting issues to resolve that they themselves had no template for, having grown up in the UK.

Peter's Story

At home in Khartoum.

Much of Peter's life in Sudan has been documented already. But there remain the challenges that he faced with family life and responsibility still to tell.

Peter took his family out to Sudan on the basis that he had acquired employment as an aircraft engineer at Khartoum Airport. But, I have been reliably informed by his Sudan Airways colleague, Alan, that he did not last long in the job before going through a mini-meltdown. Stories told by mother corroborate this. Having previously worked on light aircraft, and in fairly unorthodox fashion, it seems that Peter found it difficult to adapt to the structure and rules required when working on large, passenger aircraft. My mother went as far as to say that he was overawed by the responsibility of having to pass a large airliner, filled with people, as fit to fly. Whichever way it was, Peter was then transferred to the airline's tool sheds where he oversaw the local staff who maintained the equipment that serviced the planes. Conquering that early challenge for Peter ensured that he settled happily to his work, and life in Sudan, for the five following years.

At home Peter had settled in his young and somewhat naive wife, Joan, who had expat life to contend with. Ultimately, between him and his servant, Lawaya, he achieved this. However, there were many elements of the running of the home and family life that he had to take responsibility for himself. I feel sure that this was not something he anticipated was going to happen when he married and agreed to have a child.

It seems that household bills in Khartoum were addressed to my dad at his work. I am not sure if this was because the house did not have a postal service, or because he liked to take control of the household budget by himself. The handwritten notes at the bottom right are made by him.

Earlier in his life Peter had made clear to Joan that he did not want to have children. He was already supporting his ageing and penniless parents. Besides he wanted to be free to travel. Whilst he wanted to marry Joan he did not want to take on any further encumbrances. The birth of their first child, however, had been a pact between the two: she could have a baby if she would agree to live in Sudan, but no further children.

But then Joan contrived to get pregnant on purpose, by her own admission. Their second child was born in 1965, shortly before Peter's Sudan Airways contract was up and he was obliged to look for employment elsewhere. Now he had yet another mouth to feed, and by all accounts was furious with Joan. He settled eventually to the fact, but I feel that this period marked a turning point in his life, with several factors coming together that signalled the end of a golden era and the beginning of tough times. I remember the moment I found out that we were to be leaving Sudan. We were at the breakfast table when Dad said to Mum that he had found someone to buy our fridge. I was five years old. "Why would someone buy our fridge?" I asked. The answer that we were to be leaving Sudan shortly came, along with the news that Dad was going to work in another country called Aden. I remember feeling extremely shocked and sad at the news. But nowhere near as sad as Dad looked.

... And Other Stories

One element that dominated life at the Balkwill villa which does not fall within the scope of the personal stories were the visitors to the house. And this chapter about Khartoum life would not be complete without mention of the eclectic group of people that came by, and some of their antics.

The above image shows the first two pages of the villa's visitor book. I personally remember Schmidt, who was almost a weekly lodger, coming in to town, as he would do, for respite from the cotton spraying scheme at Al Gezira. His arrival would invariably mean partying both on the town, as well as back at the house, before collapsing to sleep in my room, from where I would have been earlier transferred to my bed on the roof.

One time he turned up unannounced, and a little the worse for wear, in the middle of the night, singing the Frank Sinatra song "Strangers in the Night" and trying to break in through the shuttered windows of my darkened bedroom. He woke me up and frightened the life out of me.

A memory that my mother shared with me from when I was a baby was of an evening that, unusually, because normally she would go out on the town, leaving me with Lawaya, she stayed home with me whilst my dad went out with several of the guys who were to be staying over. They subsequently returned from a night at the Khartoum cabaret, bringing with them a troupe of dancing girls. Naturally my mother was angry at the interruption to her quiet night in and berated my father about it when he got to bed. However, in the morning she was to explode with rage. On entering the kitchen, she found that every scrap of food in the place had been eaten, even the pureed baby food she had pre-prepared for my breakfast.

Our expat life in Khartoum could often be like that; dissolute and out of hand, reminiscent of British expat life in the 1940s in Sudan's near neighbour, Kenya, as fictionalised by James Fox in his novel "White Mischief".

But by contrast, as before described in this chapter, there was the formal entertaining at home: diplomats, businessmen, local members of the community, fellow expatriate couples from all walks of Khartoum life.

It seems that the Balkwill villa could be anything that it was required to be at any given time. And the lives of the members of the household were lived with many complexities.

Any kind of an existence back in the UK could never have matched Peter's life in his beloved Sudan. So it was with relief, no doubt, for him that he found the job in Aden, just across the Red Sea, and still within the Middle East, to move on to.

Chapter Eleven

Family Life in Aden: Drama Unfolds

The Balkwill family spends a lazy
Friday at Tarshayn Beach.

Peter Balkwill, the *Boy from the Moor*, could be forgiven, when he went to work in Aden in 1967, for his strong sense of conviction and optimism.

Sorry to have to leave a comfortable existence in Sudan after the post-colonial Sudanese government had terminated the contracts of its British expatriate workers, he had been delighted to find alternative work, and a possible future, just across the Red Sea in Aden, thus extending his life in his beloved Middle East.

At the time, Aden, having been a British colony for 127 years, was one of the busiest ports in the world and was well-connected internationally. Whilst it had been in an official state of emergency for three years since a campaign of terror had begun against its colonial rulers in 1963, it was also the case that Aden was due to be granted independence from Britain imminently. It was a thriving port city, with a valuable infrastructure and strong systems of trade, law and order, education and health that were to be inherited from the departing British. Therefore, Peter had no reason to suspect that it would not emerge, along with the protectorates of the surrounding south Yemeni hinterland, as a successful new country under local leadership. Or that he would not be well placed to take advantage of its potential good fortune, having invested his skills and good intention there at its outset.

After all, on the other side of the Arabian Peninsula from Aden, along the sparsely populated south eastern shore of the Persian Gulf, what has become in modern times the United Arab Emirates was also about to enter a loosely similar birth process. Like Aden, beginning with a British decision to withdraw — in this case, in early 1968, from its involvement in what was then the Trucial States — an agreement was made, involving local rulers Sheikh Zayed bin Sultan Al Nahyan of Abu Dhabi and Sheikh Rashid bin Saeed Al Maktoum of Dubai to found a federation. Today the UAE, which came into being in December 1971, is a modern, oil exporting country with a diversified economy, Dubai in particular being a global hub for tourism, retail and finance and having the world's tallest building and largest manmade seaport. It is likely that Peter sensed a zeitgeist at that time of decolonisation in the Middle East, but wrongly believed that what was already the successful and cosmopolitan port of Aden would be the world leader that the underdeveloped desert area of the UAE eventually became.

And I have no doubt that Peter was looking to make a life away from the UK somewhere in that central part of the world. Whilst living in Khartoum, when I was about four years old, he had taken us on a family trip to visit a former Sudan crop spraying friend of his who had bought a farm near Karen, in Kenya, East Africa. I feel strongly that he was considering doing the same. He did not act then but I think he was having similar thoughts about moving to Aden.

Whichever way, during 1967, when I was five years old, I remember him, in a state of considerable excitement, leaving us in the UK to start work in Aden. We were to join him in 1968, following independence. His phone calls home to us, always scheduled in advance and involving the entire family gathering around the single household telephone receiver to get their chance to talk with him, were always upbeat.

By contrast, as Aden's security situation began to deteriorate throughout the period, he responded by retaining his positivity and cheerfulness, and promising us that all kinds of treats and opportunities were awaiting us there.

In this respect I well remember the long-distance tussle between him and my mother. The more she would read inflammatory articles in British newspapers about violence and death in Aden, the more he would bestow promises and gifts to cajole her. For instance, the surprise of the bejewelled brooch in the shape of a *jambiya* and a gold Rolex watch. This expensive jewellery would have been courtesy of the favourable prices in what was then duty-free Aden. These would have then been further slashed as trade was plummeting, owing to the developing crisis that the colony found itself embroiled in. A particular knee jerk response I remember on the part of Mum to this charm offensive by him was to buy a puppy. In her mind this meant that we could now not possibly leave home for Aden. It was a very emotional and confusing time.

As it turned out, Dad was to be the one to win the war of emotional blackmail. The dog, a lovely cocker spaniel named Skippy, was given away, the UK house mothballed, and we found ourselves, in early January 1968, on a Middle East Airlines jet bound for Aden.

This chapter presents my experience of Aden as I remember it. My time there spanning the turning point of two years that the city, now the capital of the new country of the People's Democratic Republic of Yemen, struggled to find its way, following independence.

Coincidentally, the story of the new Aden, as it stumbled and flailed at the various political, military and economic flash points of the period, in the end turned out to be synonymous with what became the final, difficult, two years of the life of Peter Balkwill, the *Boy from the Moor*.

BRITISH TROOPS ALL PULL OUT IN R.A.F. AIRLIFT THIS MONTH

By CHAPMAN PINCHER

BRITAIN'S withdrawal from Aden is to be speeded up so that the last man should be out before the end of the month.

This was announced by Mr. Brown, the Foreign Secretary, in Parliament yesterday.

The new State of South Arabia is being left for the terrorist organisations—FLOSY (Front for the Liberation of Occupied South Yemen) and N.L.F. (National Liberation Front) to settle by themselves.

These rival factions, which have been fighting each other, are reported to have reached agreement to form a Government under the guidance of President Nasser in Cairo. But the British withdrawal is to go ahead whether a Government for South Arabia is formed or not.

PUT OFF

Britain's plans to provide protection for South Arabia against external aggression in the first six months after independence have been cancelled.

Mr. Brown said: "It is clear that the radical internationalists and other groups must face their own problems and resolve them themselves."

The Foreign Office has accepted Egyptian assurances that Colonel Nasser is withdrawing his troops from the Yemen.

So Mr. Brown believes that there is no danger of aggression against South Arabia from the Yemen, though it remains an Egyptian puppet State.

The Government is also reserving the right to cancel the three years of financial support promised to South Arabia after independence. But installations worth nearly £30 million are being abandoned with no compensation to Britain.

About 6,000 troops and civilians are to be evacuated in the biggest operation since the Berlin airlift 18 years ago. This will be carried out by the R.A.F. using VC10's, Britannias, and other transport planes.

WARSHIPS

The withdrawal may be marked by a last fling from the terrorists who feel they could then claim that they drove the British out. So a strong force of British warships is assembling.

The Commando carrier Albion, the assault ship Fearless, the frigate Phœbe, and six other naval vessels are already there. They are to be joined by the carrier Eagle and the guided missile destroyer London.

The fleet will be commanded by Rear-Admiral Edward Ashmore.

Mr. Brown's decision to speed the withdrawal from Aden foreshadows an announcement that Britain and Egypt have resumed diplomatic relations.

President Nasser is understood to have demanded recognition of the Yemen Republic by Britain as part of the diplomatic deal.

Recognition of the revolutionary Yemen Republic will sour diplomatic relations with Saudi Arabia, Kuwait, Bahrain, and other Arab States controlled by ruling families.

Saudi Arabia is Britain's biggest customer for arms. Kuwait supplies huge oil shipments to Britain and has large sterling investments. Bahrain will be Britain's only military base in the area after the withdrawal from Aden.

STEPHEN HARPER reported from Aden last night: The date of independence will be kept secret for as long as possible to forestall a build-up by Arab terrorists seeking a final battle with British troops.

A British military spokesman said: "We can leave any time between November 15 and 30."

Published on 3rd November 1967, this piece appeared in the Daily Express a matter of weeks before we left to join Dad in Aden. My mother, having read many such articles in the press throughout 1967, made the journey from our home in the UK reluctantly.

My Story
Arrival

My mother, brother and I left London Heathrow Airport on a cold, grey day in January. Mum was ambitious for me to connect with other Airwork kids on the plane. Several families of the men who had gone out with the British aviation company to work for the new South Arabian Air Force (which would then become the People's Democratic Republic of Yemen Air Force after independence) during the previous year of 1967, were at last being flown out as a contingent to join them.

Dad had briefed me excitedly on the phone that I might be travelling on a new VC10. Middle East Airlines (MEA), the Lebanon-based airline that we always flew with to and from Aden, had recently agreed to lease two of these brand new jets, one from Laker Airways, that had recently arrived, and one from Ghana Airways that was due at the end of that month. As an aircraft fanatic, he blindly assumed that I shared his passion.

As it was, evading both of my parents' wishes, I slept soundly throughout each leg of the long journey. We made stops in Geneva, Beirut and Jeddah. I distinctly remember our group's arrival in Aden, emerging out into the intense Arabian sunshine, all of us herded from the plane together. The tarmac sizzled beneath my feet. My mother had changed my stout British winter shoes with socks for open toed sandals at some stage of the journey. Our faces smarted from hot, pungent wafts emanating from aviation fuel, whilst a block of an airport building materialised ahead of us, diffused and suspended in clouds of engine vapour. We were being led there by air hostesses, who, dressed in the orange and lemon coloured uniforms of MEA, seemed to melt before us like blobs of sorbet ice cream in the gaseous atmosphere.

Our party burst into the terminal building, bringing it instantly alive. Luggage was hauled in on wooden trolleys, suitcases marked with chalk once they had been identified by their owners. A linen be-suited young man who stood alone as we entered the arrivals hall seemed to know us all. He took my little brother from my exhausted mother and arranged porters to carry everyone's luggage. All the families were transferred to a big, old, white bus waiting out the front. Years later I learned that the helpful young man was in fact a British Foreign Office official. Our collective arrival had been an official event.

An African driver, his black head beaded with sweat, swung us into gear, and our packed bus lurched forward on a journey through dusty Middle

Eastern streets lined with white stucco, flat roofed houses of distinct colonial style. I could be forgiven, at my tender age of wondrousness for believing that I was back home again in a sort of a Khartoum, a place I had been homesick for the entire previous year I had been living in the UK.

Then we rumbled into what was, apparently, our destination, a place entirely different to anything I had ever seen before. It was the Dhobi Lines compound. A former British military compound, it was a regiment of rows of three storey, drab-coloured wooden apartment blocks, standing alert on grey volcanic sand, ferociously fenced in by barbed wire and guarded by armed sentries at its gate.

As I stepped down from the bus, my father appeared as if from nowhere; his familiar big face cracked open by a wide smile. I had never before known him so pleased to see me.

It would have been a matter of about only five weeks since he had defended his ex-military apartment here through the turbulent night of Britain's withdrawal from Aden, in preparation for this arrival of ours.

Settling In

I looked around me and saw other men also embracing their family groups. Luggage was being hauled about the place. Dad was by now deep in conversation with the bus driver. It turned out that he had a special friendship with this man, who was a Sudanese immigrant to Aden. Dad obviously still felt an affinity for the people of the country that he had previously lived in for so long. And I was to come to know him well too as he, and his big, white, lumbering vehicle would figure largely throughout our daily life in Aden.

Dad led us to our apartment block. I had never before seen such a place, having only, in my short life, ever been in houses. I was therefore fascinated by the communal entrance hall, a front door to each side of us, a staircase in front of us, leading up to what apparently were more homes on top of us. There were three storeys.

As ours was a ground floor apartment, we only had to turn to our right and we were at our new front door. We entered a long, shadowy hallway. Three bedrooms lined up to the left of us, toilet and bathroom to the right. All of these rooms were very moderately sized. However, the living space that the corridor opened out onto at its end was light, airy and comfortably spacious by contrast to the sleeping quarters. There was a sitting area to the left, dining to the right. French doors opened from the dining area onto a small balcony. There was a corner bar on the opposite side of the room to the balcony doors.

Peter (left) and Joan (centre) entertain at the corner bar of the dining room in the Dhobi Lines flat.

Behind the dining room was the kitchen. There was a hatch between these two rooms. The door to the kitchen was separated off, back in the hallway. This arrangement seemed like a scaled down, modern version of the service arrangement between kitchens and dining room in the Khartoum villa that we had previously lived in, and not at all like any house I had been in the UK. The kitchen was large and filled with equipment that seemed very different to what we had had in Khartoum. The reality was that the utensils were modern, some actually quite state-of-the-art for its day, compared to the antiquated gear we had inherited at the Khartoum villa. A service balcony led from the opposite side of the kitchen to a back door that opened back onto the block's main entrance. That door stood beside our front door. In effect, the whole apartment wrapped around on itself.

We set about making ourselves at home. All around us, randomly scattered throughout the apartments of the blocks of Dhobi Lines, the other families were settling in too, seeking to find a new normal in this strange new part of the world. But life in Aden was to turn out to be anything other than ordinary. This was first evidenced for me a couple of mornings later, on the first day of school.

I had been woken exceptionally early. So early that I could see through the balcony doors, from my seat at the breakfast table, the sun still rising in a pink sky over flat salt pans to the east of us. I then had to put on a crisp white uniform dress that had been provided, somehow, before I had even arrived in the country. My mother insisted on tying my long hair up. I was given a satchel, snacks, a water bottle and, what Mum called, a sweat towel to carry with me. After my Khartoum preschool, and then infants school in the UK, my education seemed to be taking a whole new, grown-up turn.

I arrived with my mother at an assembly point alongside the compound's tall wire fence, where the big white bus was waiting. The bright light of day was by now eclipsing the mellow morning sunrise, and the scene was wakeful and lively, mothers busying over boys and girls of all ages. Our Sudanese driver opened up the door and people began to board. However, it quickly became apparent that there were not enough seats for everybody. A heated debate between the women ensued, which resulted in my mother letting go of me and me being bundled, without her, onto the bus. It later transpired that the wives of senior Airwork employees had pulled rank on the lowlier women, such as the wives of engineers, as my mother was, and claimed the limited space on the bus for themselves so as to accompany their own children to their first day at school.

In the event I remember seeing, from the bus window, Mum crying as we were driven away. Out through the compound gates and onto the road from the Dhobi Lines at Khormaksar to the school at Steamer Point, a journey of some 12 miles. I was bemused. Mum, I later learned, was deeply traumatised by the affair. As our time in Aden wore on, the long journeys to and from school were to become even more eventful and confusing for everyone involved.

Meanwhile, back at the Dhobi Lines, I understand the days were long and boring for the mothers and non-school age children left behind. The men would have gone to their jobs at the airfield. This left the women and infants, with a collection of their Somali *ayahs*, alone and with time on their hands, in the confines of the fortified compound.

156

I am not entirely clear what my mother and little brother would do all day, or who they may or may not have mixed with. I do know that she liked to cook, both British and foreign dishes. Unwilling to leave the compound for the uncertain streets of Aden alone, she could only shop intermittently for food at a supermarket for expats, the Cold Storage at Hedjuff, when my father was around to take her. Otherwise, she relied on our *ayah* to venture into Aden, usually to local Khormaksar shops, or to the *souk* in the Adeni district of Crater, for what she needed. A few vendors were allowed access to the compound. I remember, for instance, triangular shaped cartons of goat's milk, fruit (mostly bananas — we ate so many bananas in Aden), bread, cakes, bottled drinks and ice cream being delivered.

The daily torpor would be relieved for her at approximately one o'clock with the thundering and clanking of the white bus as it rolled back into the compound and parked up in its spot at the perimeter fence, just opposite where our flat was located. We school kids would pour out and disband noisily for our respective homes. Soon after that, the men would arrive home from the airfield. By 2pm the families would be sitting down to lunch at their various dining tables.

Because of the extreme heat, and humid conditions, work and school were carried out in the first half of the day. After lunch the adults would retire for a siesta, leaving us kids to roam together in the grounds of the now somewhat deserted compound. Indeed, Aden all around us would grind pretty much to a standstill, the local people withdrawing from the heat of the day to indulge in chewing qat.

Qat comes from the leaves of the Catha edulis shrub, which is native to the Arabian Peninsula and nearby Horn of Africa. The spiky-looking green leaves, when chewed like tobacco, produce feelings of euphoria. It is common throughout Yemen to see dreamy-eyed individuals, lolling, with one cheek bulging and slowly rippling as they chew on qat.

All that stirred those soporific Adeni afternoons, as I played in the compound, were kite hawks, ubiquitous in the sky above us. Black, feathery, circling blobs, rending the hot, lazy air with their cawing and their shrieking. Come late afternoon however, and the place would come alive again as our parents would wake and resume their lives again.

I'd be called in for tea. This seemed to always be toast with apricot jam. My parents, at some point, had been in receipt of a stock of leftover British forces rations. Tins of potted meat and packets of dried food. My jam, which came in tubes, looked like a sticky, gelatinous, mildly orange-coloured ointment. I suspect, as I have learned more about what had gone on in Aden in the time leading up to our arrival, that this food might have originally been part of British Army rations, meant for use by them during the various covert and dangerous missions they made into the interior in the few years before.

Mum would sit at the table with me, almost always complaining that "Jim Bang" had kept her awake again all afternoon. Jim lived in the apartment above us with his wife and large family. And they could indeed be collectively very noisy as they clattered about what would have been, with so many of them, their very compact abode. Added to that our building was wooden and prefabricated. Noise travelled easily.

One morning I arrived at the school bus to find that Jim Bang's children were not there as they should have been as usual. I came home that afternoon to be told that Jim Bang had done a flit in the night. I never knew what a "flit" was. But our home life was very peaceful thereafter. In fact, we were one of only two occupied apartments in the block at that time.

Whilst a core group of us continued to settle in Aden, a range of other people came and went. At the time of our arrival there seemed to be a variety of unknown British men that would gravitate around us Airwork families. At some point I noticed that they were no longer around. I came to learn years later that these were almost certainly a group of Royal Marines that had stayed on after the withdrawal. I am not sure why.

Jim Bang's children were not the only ones to vanish from the daily school commute. In February 1968, the brand new South Yemen Minister of Defence made a trip to Moscow, where he made a broadcast accusing "members of the South Yemen Air Force" (i.e. its British pilots) of acting as spies, and informing the British Embassy. The Yemenis were also incensed because the pilots had been instructed by the British government to stay within borders and not fly towards Saudi Arabia, in case of conflict with UK nationals flying Saudi combat patrols there. These men were subsequently called together on 27th February and told to get out with immediate effect. Under armed guard they were given one hour to collect their belongings and leave. The first the Airwork families knew about this was when the pilots' children did not show up in the morning for the bus to school. The new pilots that were subsequently recruited to take their place were a mix of Bulgarian, Yugoslav and Dutch nationals.

School

I was disgorged in a wave of the Airwork children and mothers from the white bus when we arrived at the gates of St Francis Convent, Steamer Point, on our first day of school. The girls were to attend St Francis, with its Roman Catholic church located within its compound, and the boys were to go a boy's school located just behind it.

Alone as I was, my mother having been ejected from the bus at the start of our journey, I was somehow propelled into a garden, set to the side of the main school playground and behind the church. This, it transpired, was the nursery. After a time, someone found me there, realised that at aged six I was too old for nursery, and delivered me instead to the next classroom along, off a verandah back within the main school area.

This classroom was enormous and high ceilinged, and although there were tall windows set into its back wall, it was really rather shadowy because of the dinginess of the courtyard that they gave on to. The only desk in the room was in the corner and belonged to the teacher, who was, of course, a nun. The many children in the class sat in rows on the floor. Surprisingly, since this was a girl's school, there were boys in this class. Most of the children were ethnic Adenis and subcontinental Indians.

I joined the kids on the floor and learnt quickly that this was an environment where one had to pay attention at all times. We were being taught entirely from the black board and by rote. We were required to chant a great deal. Should a child lapse concentration or fall behind then there would always be consequences. A sharp rap on the palm of the hand with a wooden ruler in the first instance, or having to stand, face into a corner of the room, and called a dunce for more severe transgressions. Of course it was a case of personal pride and competition amongst the boys to see who could be sent to the corner the most.

Although I always tried to remain quiet and alert in this class, I did not escape punishment. I remember receiving a thwack of the ruler at least once during that time. This came from the visiting Arabic language teacher. She was a very sophisticated and beautiful lady. She was quite young and had a bee hive hairdo, as was the fashion of the Western world of the time. She wore exotic make up and jewellery and Western dress. I imagine that she hailed from Lebanon or one of the countries of the Levant. Well, one day she caught me idling and staring out of one of the windows when I should have been chanting Arabic vocabulary. The embarrassing thing for me when I was asked to explain what I was looking at is that I was actually scrutinising the school's toilet block. This low-level, three door building stood in the back yard behind the classroom. Two of the doors, which led to the toilets we were allowed to use, gave onto Middle Eastern-style, hole-in-the-ground, toilets. The third door was to a cubicle, which contained a Western-type toilet pan, which was for use by older girls and staff. For some reason I found this differentiation between toilets fascinating and wondered why everyone didn't just use the same type of toilet.

Anyway, I didn't last long in that first class. It turned out that, having already learned to read and write earlier in my life, I had the ability to be in a class higher, but for one thing. Whilst I could write, I had not yet learned how to do joined-up writing. Once I had, somehow, learned that particular skill from the blackboard of the enormous first classroom, I was moved to a new class in a small room off a side courtyard of the school, to the other side of the playground from the nursery. The interior of this room was even darker than the last. It had only a small, ceiling height window in its back wall, which I believe gave out onto a street. Rows of old-fashioned wooden desks faced a black board at the front of the room. All of the pupils here were girls. I sat at the front with an Adeni girl called Maktab. The teacher was a kindly nun, who I believe was Irish because she always said "tree" instead of "three", in an Irish kind of a way. Almost all of the nuns, however, were Italian.

Again, I remained a short while, before being transferred to a larger classroom across the courtyard. This class was so short of natural light that it was positively murky. There were only a few pupils here and we all sat near the door, presumably so that we could at least see. I didn't know why I had been moved here. Maktab, for instance, had remained in the previous class. But I do know that this was the class where we first began to learn arithmetic. There was a lot of chanting of times tables here.

I finished my days at St Francis in an upstairs classroom, off a balcony above the arithmetic classroom. A room that seemed quite bathed in sunlight, compared to the previous ones I had frequented. It had floor-to-ceiling windows that were open to the balcony, allowing fresh morning sunlight to pour in from the sky immediately above us. Here we seemed to learn more esoteric subjects. There was no chanting; instead we would discuss religion, history, geography and poetry. We would sing a lot, at the top of our voices and without musical accompaniment. We learned embroidery, which I loved, and occasionally, we would be taken into the main playground for PT (physical training). This involved standing in rows in front of a nun, dressed in her full regalia of a crisp white habit and veil, and jumping up and down, and bending and squatting, fully clothed in uniform dresses. It was just like a military drill.

The St Francis complex was of old colonial design. Built around a series of courtyards, with maximum flow of air and provision of shade in mind. We wore white in order to reflect the heat, and our dresses, made of cotton, sat lightly on our skin. Nevertheless, we kids could get very hot and sweaty. We carried water bottles and a sweat towel. In particular the sweat towel would come in very handy to sit on on the plastic seats of the white bus. Should the sweaty flesh of our legs have direct contact with the plastic for any length of time during the hot and humid midday bus ride home, then we would be apt to get stuck to the seats and a raw welt would develop across the backs of our legs.

St Francis Convent School photographed in 1996. Since I was a pupil there in 1968–69 the playground has been divided by the brick-built wall shown here. My first classroom, in which I had to sit on the floor, chanting, is behind the wall to the right of the picture, beneath the tree.

We also carried snacks of fruit, cake and sandwiches to eat at break. A local lady would appear at this time and sit in the shade of the verandah in front of my first classroom selling boiled sweets and candy from a wicker basket. Chocolate was an absolute no-no as it would have melted instantly. After school, vendors would appear at the gate selling nuts and other treats to tempt us homeward-bound kids. We would have one break time during the morning. By lunchtime we would be finished for the day and ready to go home. The Airwork kids would wait together behind a huge bulletproof fence for the Sudanese driver to pull up outside in the big white bus. He would be accompanied by an Airwork mother. These women had a rota for this duty and were responsible for ensuring that all the kids got safely home to the compound at Khormaksar.

Leisure Time
There was only one full day off per week in Aden. This was the Muslim holy day of Friday. Sunday was a half day, i.e. half of a morning.

On Fridays, Airwork laid on our ever-present white bus to ferry the families to the beach. The beach in question was Tarshayn Beach, which was located some way round Aden peninsula from our homes at the Dhobi Lines at Khormaksar, just beyond Steamer Point.

Up until the recent British withdrawal, Tarshayn had been a forces officers' beach. There were purpose-built shelters on the sand, various club house buildings, a swimming pool behind that, and officers' housing to the back of that, where the track from the Steamer Point road came in. But all of these buildings were utterly abandoned. The swimming pool devoid of water. The empty officers' quarters hollow and eerie.

Leaving the adults to picnic or snooze, we kids never quite knew whether it was more fun to jump in the surf that crashed onto the beach or scour for beautiful Indian Ocean shells that the waves threw onto its sand. Or indeed, when the adults weren't looking, break into the club buildings. There we found signs of recent abandonment: a fully stocked industrial kitchen and tools in the pool maintenance room. Changing rooms, mess rooms and so on. So much fun when you are only six years old.

One Friday, the Airwork bus turned up at Tarshayn and, on alighting, we found the entire place had been vandalised. The raffia roofs of the shelters torn apart, contents of the club buildings strewn everywhere, chairs and tables thrown in the sea. And the shark nets cut. Apparently this had all been done after a night of anti-British sentiment in Aden, although I am not sure what event had been the cause of such fervent feeling. Anyway, once the shark nets had been cut, the decision was taken, for the safety of the families that the bus service to the beach would no longer operate. After that the families made their own provision for Friday leisure time. The Balkwill family chose to buy membership of a private beach club named Gold Mohur, situated a little further round the peninsula, and which was safely fenced in by a shark net.

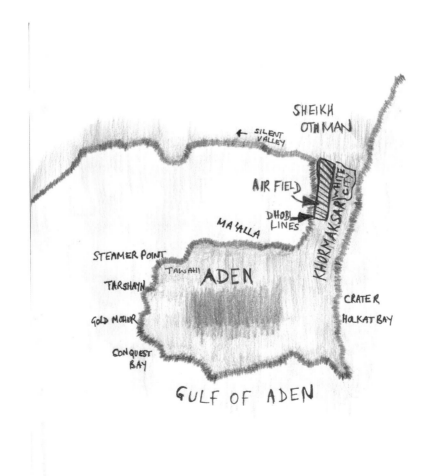

Whilst Fridays for families were spent at the beach, I gather that adults without children liked to spend their free day playing golf. I understand that there were courses at Khormaksar and Little Aden, with fairways composed of hard baked sand for grass.

Occasionally a special day trip would be planned for our one day off a week. One Friday, my brother and I were told that we were going for a special treat. We were woken early and then set off in the family Fiat 500 car. A group of colleagues of Airwork and friends followed us. Dad went in a direction I had never been before. Turning off the Khormaksar to Ma'alla road, he drove along a causeway that cut across the salt pans that lay to the east of the Dhobi Lines flats, where flamingoes lived. I was surprised to be going this way as I had always considered it a road to nowhere, leading as it seemed to do, into an empty, shimmering horizon. However, as we travelled on we reached a whole new landmass of sweeping plains, jagged peaks, and roadside dwellings that I had never imagined before existed beyond the horizon. This was a twin peninsula to Aden, named Little Aden. And we were destined for the British Petroleum installation there.

Opened in 1954 the BP site, which, surprisingly, since this was after the British had been so gleefully rejected at independence, was still British-operated at the time of our visit. I believe BP continued to be run by the British until it was sold to the PDRY Government in 1977. It was a town of its own in the wilderness. It encompassed the refinery, which was its reason for being, several housing estates where its predominately British multi-national staff lived and all the facilities they might require. BP even had its own hospital.

But we were headed for the company's social and beach club, the Bureika Club. Seemingly my father, or one of the colleagues that accompanied us, knew someone at BP who had facilitated this day out. And we had a great time. This was a brand new, shark net fenced beach for us to discover, with all kinds of purpose-built attractions. After swimming we sat down to eat a slap-up lunch in the beachside restaurant. Everything about the Bureika Club seemed genteel and somewhat privileged, compared to the conditions we were living in across the causeway in revolutionary Aden. It was a world apart and I arrived back at the White City that evening feeling serene.

On another free Friday, my family and one or two Airwork people were treated by the local businessman who, at the time, owned the Gold Mohur beach club, to a picnic at the al-Husseini Gardens in upcountry Lahej.

We set off in a convoy. The journey from the Aden peninsula, through Sheikh Othman and up to mainland south Yemen, was unnecessarily long, being punctuated at time-consuming intervals by numerous roadblocks at which our vehicles were thoroughly searched. I remember being amazed that my parents had taken the decision to travel like this at all. It seemed almost as though we were voluntarily embroiling ourselves in the hostility and mayhem of the febrile streets of Aden which we, thus far, had managed to avoid by existing in fortified compounds, and gliding through trouble to only recognised destinations in our official white bus or in the low-key vehicles that we owned.

But the sight and sounds of Lahej, when we eventually got that far, immediately distracted me from any negative thoughts. I had had no idea, during the year or so that I had been contained in compact, urban Aden, that this place existed beyond the natural barrier of jagged, volcanic peaks that truncated my miniature world of Aden from everything beyond. This traditional Arabian land of mud-built villages, of a date palm-dotted countryside being worked using camels and donkeys, and of the fantastical Arabian Nights-style Lahej Palace. Until the recent expulsion at independence by the Socialist regime enforced by the sitting South Yemeni (Abdali) Sultan, the palace had been occupied by the Sultans of Lahej, who were a dynasty that dated, through a mixed history, back to 1728.

Arriving at al-Husseini Gardens, I was entranced. I had never seen anything so tropical. Immediately our host set about having workers cut down large, flat, green banana leaves from trees nearby to lay on the ground as a make-shift picnic blanket for us all to sit on.

An arrangement of banana leaves on the ground served as the picnic blanket at our 1969 upcountry picnic at Lahej.

Our host made a show of eating a fruit straight from a tree (it was a papaya, I think). And he sent men up tree trunks to fetch fresh dates for us to eat at our picnic. For a child of seven, it was a magical day.

There were also activities at the former British mess, by now in the hands of the SYAF. I watched a cricket match in the grounds there. There was a bar popular with adults, and various night time parties were held there.

Airwork employees enjoy leisure time at the bar of the SYAF mess.

Also, films were shown on the terrace for children in the afternoons and evenings; "Monte Carlo or Bust" is one I remember. On one occasion I went to the local outdoor cinema to see "The Sound of Music". However, by the time the latest James Bond film (I can't remember which one) arrived in Aden to be shown there, my parents considered the security situation to be too unsafe to attend. It was the case that snipers had operated amongst the mixed cinema audience of locals and Brits during the days of the official state of emergency of British Aden, which, in our day, made the cinema an ominous place for us in times of trouble. I believe braver Airwork families did attend, however. Parties were held in private homes for the Airwork children, and I remember, at Christmas 1968, attending a kids' party at the British Embassy, where I won a prize at musical chairs!

We All Move House

One day, approximately six months after our arrival in Aden, I was sitting at the table of the Dhobi Lines flat, having got home from school and waiting for my lunch, when Dad burst in in a state of high excitement. "Guess who's got the bar!" he yelled right at my mother. I saw the expression of surprise and bewilderment on her face. And I was pretty shocked too at this sudden exuberance. Before she could utter anything he had told her: "WE HAVE!"

Neither Mum nor I understood what he was on about. But as I saw him explain to her that it was a former RAF officer's house in the White City, across the road from the Dhobi Lines, which had in its living room a full-size bar with all the features, I saw comprehension dawn on her face. And this was the first I learnt, as they had previously neglected to inform me, that we would imminently be moving house.

The White City was, like the Dhobi Lines, a fenced in compound. Unlike the barrack-like accommodation of the Dhobi Lines that had been hastily put together from flat pack sometime late in the British tenure of Aden, the White City was a grid of elegant, 1930s white painted houses. Each house was designed with slightly different Art Deco features to its neighbour. All were very well appointed and designed for comfort inside.

My mother gasped when she first saw the interior of our house during a preliminary visit a couple of days later. Not because it contained the full-size bar in its living room that had so excited Dad, but because it had a downstairs toilet. She had, of course, grown up in the UK without so much as an indoor toilet, let alone the luxury of WC facilities on both the ground and upper floors.

I clearly remember entering the Sloane Street house that first time. Despite there being items of furniture scattered round, the place echoed. Local workers were busying themselves throughout the rooms. The air smelt of chemicals that suggested cleaning products and paint. We entered the kitchen area, and it reminded me faintly of the Sudan villa. It came in two parts. The cooking area was divided on the one side by an enormous walk-in pantry, and a breakfast room on the other side. A built-in dresser lined one wall of the breakfast room, which was nothing short of a beautiful feat of Art Deco carpentry. Even though I didn't know what it was then, I recognised that this was a unique artistic style.

From the kitchen Dad manoeuvred us towards his precious bar. It had its own door off the hall area, which he disappeared through. We saw him again on the other side of it, after we had walked through the formal dining area into a spacious lounge. He stood there beaming at us, asking us what we wanted to drink as a joke.

I looked around the room and saw big windows with billowing curtains, also reminiscent of the Khartoum house. French doors led out to the front side onto a verandah. Although it was much smaller than at the Khartoum house, the verandah looked nevertheless lovely and shady. Looking upwards, I saw that the ceiling was heavily marked with brown stains.

Years later Mum explained to me that the highly stained sitting room ceiling of the Sloane Street house was the result of wanton vandalism at the time of independence. This was not, incidentally, by way of anti-British feeling on the part of the incoming Adenis, as I had seen to be the case at Tarshayn, but actually caused by the departing British.

Apparently there had been a night at the Sloane Street house, immediately before the withdrawal, when the entire stock of the bar, which had, at that point, been being used as an officers' club, was destroyed. Champagne and beer had flowed and fizzed. Shaken right up and spurted at the ceiling from the bottles. Spoil any valuable goods that couldn't be taken away as well as damage the remaining infrastructure.

I understand that, at the time, similar events were occurring all around Aden. Files and records being shredded and burned. A, perhaps apocryphal, story I have heard concerns a British serviceman who could not sell his car before leaving. Rather than give it away or just abandon it to lucky new owners, he had it helicoptered onto one of the volcanic peaks that rise up over Aden to sit there, far out of reach by anyone on foot.

Interiors and furniture had been smashed up too. And this was why, Mum explained, we had had to wait the several months at the flats to move into the White City: time for the houses to be renovated and furniture to be found for us.

We went upstairs, the staircase being another beautifully fashioned wooden feature of the house, as the breakfast room dresser had been. The bedrooms were lovely and large. My parents had a room at the front that gave onto a balcony with porthole features that gave the impression from externally that the house was an ocean-going liner. I was enchanted to see that one wall of my bedroom was curved rather than having a corner angle. The bathroom was tiled throughout and had not only a huge roll top bath, but also a separate shower cubicle. I had never seen a standalone shower before.

Looking out of my bedroom window at the front of the house, Dad explained to me that his colleague and friend lived opposite us. To each side lived Adeni Air Force employees. Dotted down Sloane Street, on both sides, lived fellow British Airwork families.

Our White City house.

The following week or so saw our Dhobi Lines flat as a hive of activity, as Mum busily packed up our belongings in readiness for the move. She also insisted upon cleaning the place from top to bottom. As we all knew that the property was going to be given over to incoming local families from upcountry, and I had seen my mother's increasing irritation with these people who had been swarming into Aden and causing chaos, I expressed surprise that she cared so much on their behalf. For that I earned a thorough telling off and a lecture about always maintaining standards.

Anyway, one day, instead of dropping us back to the Dhobi Lines from school, the white bus cranked on past that compound and in through the gates of the White City, dropping us kids at the various houses, in different streets, that had been allocated to our families. And there was Mum, in our Sloane Street house, waiting for me with everything in place. Years later she told me that, after I had left the flat for school that morning, a donkey and cart had arrived to ferry our belongings to our new abode.

Politics: The Human Experience

As my mother remembered it, the situation in Aden was never anything other than tense, right from the start of our time there. Her and my collective memory is of a dysfunction underpinning our daily lives that was much bigger than anything we could understand or make sense of. On arrival, the chaos, danger and abandonment of the preceding weeks, months and years of the fight for, and process of, independence were very apparent in our immediate surroundings. Unless one personally experiences it, it is hard to truly know what it is like living the legacy of seismic global events, and how it affects ordinary people's everyday existence. What had been homes in Aden now stood empty, paint peeling and infrastructure falling apart. This only a matter of a month since the British withdrew. Patches of foliage, that had, probably generations before, been planted in volcanic earth to grace door fronts and shade verandahs, had, without attention, quickly turned to barren twigs instead. Ropes hung from each of the upper floor balconies of the Dhobi Lines apartment blocks. Inauspicious and looking like hangman's nooses, I understand that these ropes had been installed for quick getaway by the British at the withdrawal.

Indeed, on first arriving in Aden and living at the Dhobi Lines (i.e. in the first half of 1968), the Airwork families were required themselves to be prepared for evacuation at all times. To that end, each family had to keep one suitcase packed with their bare essentials. Mum joked for years afterwards that the Balkwill suitcase was filled entirely with nappies for my baby brother and toys for me. But of course, this wasn't really a laughing matter and she was constantly anxious at the time. And with good reason, it turned out. Because on one occasion we actually were given the signal to flee.

I have some memory of the event, but the finer detail has been pieced together from what my mother has told me. It was midday or afternoon time, and we were all together in the flat. Mum and Dad were rushing about. I was told we were leaving, but not more than that. I grabbed a doll to take with me. We left our home and bundled, with other families, onto the waiting white bus. Several of the Airwork guys were directing us. It had been a long-rehearsed operation by them, my mum later told me. She remembered them then cutting the compound wire fence with bolt cutters to let the bus through, however I just remember us being quickly on the road towards Steamer Point. We kept going through what I thought were normal-looking Aden (by Aden standards) streets, which was surprising to me, as I had by now been told that we were in a crisis. Eventually we left the main road and trundled down the track to Tarshayn Beach, where we all piled out of the bus. It was still daylight and I took myself off to sit down as others milled about the beach. I sat there for ages, fully clothed and cuddling my doll in a place I had always known for playing, carefree, in the sea and on the sand in my swimsuit. Everyone was talking about, and pointing at, a ship that had appeared off shore from our lonely spot. I later learned that this was a British naval ship come specifically to evacuate us. However, as it turned out, it was decided that we would not leave and we all trooped back onto the bus, arriving back at the Dhobi Lines tired and hungry for tea that evening.

An epidemic of stray cats roamed the domestic compounds, former pets of the British, now seeking out a new home, or at least a hand to feed them. Masses of desperate-looking Somali women would besiege my mother, whenever they could get near her, begging for work with us children. For generations these women had been coming to good jobs in Aden with British service families, now they were very suddenly unemployed and bereft.

A matter of contention in the Balkwill household during the early weeks of life at the Dhobi Lines was me playing, unsupervised, with the other Airwork kids, out in the compound in the afternoons. I was made to promise my parents again and again that I would not join my gang of playmates in breaking into the several empty and abandoned flats within the compound. This promise I would solemnly undertake, then go right out and disobey them. It was such fun to me, and seemed so harmless.

The reality, I learned years later, was that my parents were worried that I could get shot. It seems that, because of the amount of looting that had gone on at independence, the sentries that guarded the Dhobi Lines were under orders to shoot on sight anyone found breaking into property. My mother, probably with good reason, embellished this story as she told it to me in her old age with her personal memory of routinely seeing the compound's armed guards, waving their ferocious-looking weapons around whilst simultaneously being high on qat. Thus, she considered them incapable of being able to distinguish between a looter and an innocent child. In the event none of us did get shot.

Across the road at the White City after our move, however, we kids did face another hostile challenge, which was very immediate. This again came from events entirely outside of our making, and was very immediate. Unlike at the Dhobi Lines, which was entirely occupied by British people, the White City was a mix of notable Adeni families as well as the British. Most of these locals were friendly towards us. The adults, in particular, understood our reason for being in Aden. However, some of their children, grown up on a diet of violence towards the British in Aden during the recent time of occupation, could be very aggressive towards us. I remember at times, we kids running for what we felt was our lives from local children coming after us, throwing stones. On more than one occasion, someone got hit.

I have already written about the time that the beach club at Tarshayn was vandalised. That was an immediate and shocking experience. However, what I saw unfolding in the streets of Aden from the window of the white bus as we travelled to and from school each day was more a visual diary of the ongoing destruction of newly independent Aden.

Initially, the long, straight road through Ma'alla called not so imaginatively the Ma'alla Straight, appeared as a tidy, modern dual carriageway, lined on either side by neat blocks of pastel-painted flats with busy shops at their ground floor levels. It is hard to compare this place to anywhere else I have seen in the world, with its British-style buildings set in a Middle Eastern surrounding. Ma'alla had been, in antiquity, a village made up of African peoples, dhow-builders (a dhow being a traditional wooden-built boat), fishermen and caravaneers before the British came and shored it up, largely obscuring it from its waterfront with the long rows of apartments blocks and shops that they built there in which to accommodate their own, and other, expatriate workers.

The flats, when I first saw them, were clearly predominantly empty, but they seemed maintained and expectant of careful new owners at any time. In the event however, what I actually saw was a random colonisation take place. Huge extended families taking possession of modest-sized dwellings, as and when, spilling out onto the front balconies where belongings were piled so precariously that they could fall onto the street at any moment. Live goats peered down from those lofty heights. Rubbish piled up in the streets below, having emanated from the front doors of the apartment block stairwells.

During the early days of the school bus journey, I would see many children of the Indian community going about their day alongside the Ma'alla Straight. On their religious high days and holidays, they would line the road, cheering and dressed in colourful, shiny clothing. Increasingly though they disappeared from the scene. I assume because they were the children of the Straight's Indian shopkeepers who were increasingly closing down their once busy businesses and moving on to more stable parts of the world.

As we would pass our former homes at the Dhobi Lines at the start of our journeys to school, we saw similar degradation. In no time at all, the apartment blocks there became completely dishevelled after we left them. Knowing this, when I went back to take a look there on my 1996 revisit to Aden, I was stunned to see these buildings still standing. But only just. What was really noticeable then was the amount of these flat-pack, wooden apartments that were scorch-marked or fire damaged. It was explained to me that this was because Bedouin families from upcountry had moved into the properties and proceeded to light camp fires in their interiors.

Before (1968) and after (1996): the Dhobi Lines apartments. In the 1968 photo the rope that hangs from the top balcony had been placed there for quick escape at the British evacuation of November, 1967. As described in this chapter, we Airwork families performed an aborted evacuation in 1968. The rope would not have been used then as no-one was living in the top flat at that time.

Rolling through Ma'alla towards school at Steamer Point, looking up out of the bus windows to our left, one would see an expanse of dirty brown volcanic rock reaching into the sky. We kids knew that somewhere behind this formidable, barren frontier lay, what was to us the fabled, township of Crater. A place of which we were in awe.

Until the British arrived in 1839, Aden was no more than a native village, nestling in a volcanic crater. By the mid-1850s, whilst urban settlement was beginning to sprawl in areas beyond, the town inside the volcano now covered a large area, boasting many British-built public buildings. This new district called Crater, with right-angled streets featuring buildings of grey and black stone, rather than traditional earthen or brick Yemeni architecture, came to resemble more of a northern British city than a Middle Eastern settlement. However, a thriving *souk*, animal market and Indian temples, synagogues and mosques remained, fusing British imperial orderliness with the various cultures of its Empire, everyone existing cheek by jowl together. And by the time an official emergency had been imposed by the British authorities, in the last violent years before their withdrawal just before the time of our school bus journeys, Crater had become a bustling melting pot. Here intrigue and subterfuge against the colonial overlords were being fomented by local insurgents, the infamous Keeni Meeni squads operated and British people were being routinely assassinated amid the chaos.

Crater, photographed in 1996: a fusion of British imperial orderliness with the cultures of its Empire, all contained inside a volcano.

Because of this recent history, Crater was deemed unsafe for the few British people living in Aden immediately after the withdrawal, and few of them ventured there. Most of us kids never went there at all. Our Somali *ayahs* could go there, however, and we were joined daily in school by Adeni children who had come in from their homes in Crater. But we British kids were left only to imagine what this supposedly hostile, teeming cauldron of a place must be like. I eventually went there for the first time as an adult in 1996. Initially in awe of its history and with trepidation because of its reputation, I soon relaxed and began to enjoy its lively street life and friendly people, who all wanted to chat to the first British people they had come across in over two decades.

Trundling through the Crescent area one morning, on our long journey to school at Steamer Point, I saw, below my bus window, a gunfight being played out in the gardens there. Looking back, it is bizarre to think that I was a seven-year-old not frightened by this sight. Instead I just looked at the scene with curiosity. So much had happened around me by that point of my time in Aden that I had become inured to such things. Indeed, our unswerving Sudanese driver propelled us on from there, delivering us at the school gates on time for lessons as if nothing at all untoward had happened on our journey.

On another occasion, we were sitting in school when a set of huge explosions rocked us until our teeth jangled. We were in the dingy maths classroom at the time. Although we were all by now quite used to the sounds and sights of hostilities in our lives, we knew immediately that this sudden cacophony signalled something rather more sinister. Nevertheless obedient, we looked across to the nun at her teacher's desk for direction as to what to do next. "Get under your desks", she urged in a quiet, measured voice, so we did. From there, peering round desk legs through the gloom, I caught a comical glimpse of the nun, prone face down on the ground, the mass of her gleaming white habit shimmering in the darkness beyond.

Somehow that emergency ended for the day and the Airwork kids were herded from their various classrooms. The boys joined us from the school behind. We remained in the securely fenced-in playground long after all the local girls had left for home. Eventually a minibus arrived to pick us up. It was my father who was at the wheel. Everybody was tense, and the minibus, so much smaller than our usual white bus, was jam-packed. Dad drove us all home to the White City at Khormaksar on a journey that was spent almost in complete silence.

Years later my mother told me, rightly or wrongly, that no-one else at the compound would agree to make the 12 mile or so trip through Aden's strife-torn streets to collect us that day.

One time the Airwork families were indirectly affected in Aden by violence caused by wider Middle Eastern politics. We were due to be going home on leave, all set to depart on a particular day together, travelling with Middle East Airlines (MEA) as usual, via Beirut. But, when the time came, we received word that the most part of the MEA passenger fleet had been blown up at Beirut International Airport. I was told nothing of the specifics at the time. Researching for this book I have discovered that the incident took place during the evening of 28th December 1968, which is strange, as we usually took our leave during the British summer months, and I am not sure why we would have been travelling at that time of year on that occasion. 12 passenger planes belonging to MEA were blown up by Israeli commandos in an operation codenamed "Operation Gift". This was in response to an attack, two days earlier, on Israeli El Al flight 253 by the Lebanon-based Palestinian militant organisation Popular Front for the Liberation of Palestine. 9G–ABP, the VC10 on loan from Ghana Airways that I mentioned at the start of this chapter, was one of the planes involved. The late 1960s was a period when Middle Eastern politics was hotting up and beginning to involve acts of violence and terrorism, something which Aden was very soon going to be playing a supporting role in.

Back in Aden, during the most extreme events that occurred, we did not leave our compound at all, for school or anything else. This first happened when we were living at the Dhobi Lines, and again later on in the White City. On those occasions everyone would spend the long days just hanging around home.

Playmates in the White City compound.

I knew that one emergency, that occurred whilst we were living at the White City, must be more serious than any that had gone before because we stayed, on that occasion, caged in the compound for many days. I feel like it was this event that caused Aden, and our lives there, to deteriorate at such a quickening pace, and in so spectacular a fashion, that it was the catalyst that brought about the end of Airwork's time there.

On that occasion I remember a series of coffee mornings hosted by my mother, when various Airwork women came to discuss, at length, what might or might not be transpiring beyond the confines of the White City. Huddled at the living room bar, Dad and his colleagues did the same. Excluded and uninterested, I remember at one point during this tedious episode chasing about the house with a fly swat (flies were an absolute menace in Aden) because I was so bored. And then getting into trouble afterwards for having messed the walls with gruesome patches of the splatted insects.

Another time during this period I was sent out with the *ayah* to play. She took me several houses away to meet up with one of her fellow *ayah* friends who was minding other kids that I knew. We had a blast together, as was always the case in my experience, when spending time with the *ayahs.* On returning home I found that my parents had been having a party. It was still daylight and people were staggering about all over the place (I saw one man walk into a wall), which was when I first fully found out what being very drunk looked like. Later on in life my mum talked to me about that afternoon.

Seemingly someone had got hold of a copy of a recording of the single "Hey Jude", which had been released several months earlier, and the assembled company of my dad, his colleagues and my mother laid about in the sitting room listening to it over and over. They had been hearing about this latest Beatles song for some time from contacts in the UK and now finally they were listening to it in Aden. By all accounts they considered it ground breaking and spent time discussing it at length. The booze from our bar flowed, and filled that one of the many soporific afternoons of that period for them.

Eventually life resumed. I wouldn't say "back to normal", because, as before said, Aden seemed, from thereon in, in decline. And daily life in the compound was definitely on the crazy side of normal.

One day I got home from school to find my mum and brother relating excitedly how a helicopter had landed on the flat roof of the house next door. The air force pilot neighbour had come home for lunch, Mum explained. Another time I got off the school bus to see an enormous American car, its roof rolled back, gleaming in the midday sun outside the house of the man who lived opposite. As I understand it, that man did not even have a driving licence. He'd bought the car because he could, because it was going dirt cheap as the businesses of the boom time of British Aden were closing everywhere.

At play in the compound talk amongst the kids turned to the subject of sex. We all knew of it, Playboy magazines were everywhere in our daily lives. Older kids seemed to know which adults around us were doing it with each other. Not all the combinations were logical. Two successive *ayahs* of ours that were sacked around that time, I later learned, had been caught selling sex from the *tukal* behind our house to people my father knew.

Life was just getting madder and madder. When I read about the chaotic last days of World War II in Berlin as a teenager I was put in mind of those revolutionary and anarchic days in Aden of my childhood. When all was about to be lost and inhibitions let go with it.

One quiet afternoon, sitting out on the verandah after lunch, Mum and I could suddenly hear, advancing towards us from somewhere within the house, my father, who was yelling. Then he appeared through the curtains of the French windows so dramatically that this could have been a stage entrance by him and we his audience. His face contorted with pain and fear, he was holding his arm in the air, blood spurting everywhere. Mum rushed him inside. A neighbour was summoned and Dad was taken by him to hospital, where his wound was stitched up. He then returned home and explained to us what had happened. He had been in the walk-in larder at the back of the house when he saw a fly buzzing about the food in there. Then, somehow, in his enthusiasm to swat this dirty pest, he managed to crash his arm through the larder window, severing veins in his wrist. He felt foolish about this and set about getting back on with his life speedily following his return from hospital. However, it was not long before he was to discover that the site of his wound had turned gangrenous and he was soon on a plane bound for the UK for vital surgery to save his arm.

Dad leaving us alone in Aden at that time brought us all to the most searing realisation that our family life had by now become precarious almost beyond belief.

The *ayah* moved in to the house from the *tukal* to keep us company, but nothing could contain our mother's anxiety, and we kids truly felt it. I don't know how long this situation went on, but I do remember Dad eventually returning, bringing with him chocolate that we had to eat instantly before it melted.

I was next to suffer an injury. A cut on my foot that turned septic and which would stubbornly not be ameliorated, given the humid conditions and volcanic dirt that filtered into it through my open-toed sandals every day. At school we British kids were suddenly banned from learning Arabic, so we were left spending silly amounts of time just reading English language comics at the back of classrooms whilst the real business of school carried on without us. At home one day, I remember, watching with bewilderment and resentment, Dad, at the breakfast room table. Somewhat hysterically, he was dissecting a choc ice which a boy admirer of mine had brought round for me from a local vendor. Stabbing and slicing. I was never given an explanation as to why Dad would do this, and assume now that it was because he feared that the ice cream might have contained poison. Such had become the lapse of trust between Brits and locals. At the age of only seven, I felt I was losing all structure and civility from my life.

Eventually I was told that we would be leaving Aden, all the families together. The situation had become intolerable for us. The men would stay to finish the PDRSY Airwork contract and then move on to other overseas postings.

And the end was immediate. We packed all that we could carry in suitcases, everything else being left to be shipped. We all departed the compound for the airport together. I cannot for the life of me remember how we got there, whether this was or was not my last journey on the old white bus. What I do remember is that it was early morning and we all sat on the airfield together waiting for, and then watching, the plane that was coming to fetch us approaching out of the big empty, faraway sky. It landed in front of us, and we boarded it, all without ever going into the terminal building.

Jeddah, Beirut, Geneva, it was a merry return journey. Beirut, I remember, being particularly striking. The Balkwill family had transited here before, and had even stayed over in the city on one occasion. I always thought of it as the place where the Middle Eastern side of my life met the west of my European homeland. And in those days, before the war broke out in 1975 that rocked Lebanon for so long, it was quite the glamorous destination. "Paris of the Middle East" they used to call it. We flew in over the Corniche, where the sparkling blue Mediterranean Sea met the palm tree-lined shore. Trooping from the airliner to the bright white terminal building, we were met by a sign that welcomed us in no less than three languages: "Welcome to Lebanon", "Bienvenue au Liban" and the same in Arabic. Inside the terminal they spoke to us in French, giving us plastic transit cards. We were then free to wander at will, amongst sharply dressed Lebanese men and women, in the airport's chic shops, or, as most of our crowd did, head for the bars. It all seemed so civilised after so many months spent in Aden.

The Airwork group was happy and relieved to be returning "home" to the UK. None more so than my mother.

Post Script: Happily, my foot healed very quickly following my return to the temperate climate of the UK.

Death

Last known photo of Peter '*Boy from the Moor*' Balkwill. Taken on the verandah of the White City house in late 1969.

My father came briefly to settle us back in at home in the UK. I remember him accompanying me on a visit to my new school, as well as the leaving present (which I still have today) of a musical box that plays "Around the World I've Searched for You", a Nat King Cole song, which seems oddly poignant now, given that I have spent numerous subsequent years searching for him abroad and at home.

And I remember him leaving the house one blustery, autumn day to return to Aden. Just a short trip to finish off the contract, he told us. His next Airwork posting was already organised, to begin in early 1970, in Abu Dhabi.

My mother told me late in her life that she accompanied him to the bus station in town that day, from where he was to travel to the airport. She said he was exceedingly nervous, and turned to her, before boarding the bus, to ask her if she thought he was "doing the right thing" in going. They decided together that he should go. She never explained why he might have been so nervous that day. And that was, of course, the last time she saw him. Just over a month later we were to receive a visit and letter informing us that he had been killed.

Politics: The Actual Backdrop

I have no idea how the revolutionary events of our two years spent in Aden actually correlate with the Balkwill family experiences there. I was too young to know at the time, and am unable to properly work it out in adulthood. Even my mother, before she died, could not make any sense of it for me.

The only way to even begin to comprehend just how our personal lives were affected by, and intertwined with, the new South Yemen's struggle at independence is to present the historical timeline of that two-year period and then imagine ourselves contained within the story.

Timeline of South Yemen at Independence: events leading up to, and including, 1968–1969

The People's Republic of South Yemen (PRSY) came into existence on 30th November 1967, sweeping away over a century of British colonial rule, and replacing it with the only Marxist state to ever have existed in Arabia.

The Federation of South Arabia had only been formed in 1959 out of the tribal lands of the south Yemen interior. The sophisticated port city of Aden had reluctantly joined in January 1963, following the outbreak of the Egyptian-backed North Yemeni revolution of 1962. The original reason for forming the federation was to enable Britain to leave but retain its base in Aden, a plan that had been abandoned in 1966, as well as keeping a friendly government in place, a strategy that also failed since what ultimately happened was that a succession of hostile regimes took power. What was actually the case, however, was that the collection of emirates, sultanates and sheikhdoms were unruly and mismatched and so failed to form a credible nation state. During the final months of British rule, two factions, FLOSY (Front for the Liberation of Occupied South Yemen) and NLF (National Liberation Front), having previously focused on killing their British overlords, fought viciously against each other in the streets of Aden as well as in its surroundings for control at independence. In the event the NLF triumphed over FLOSY, who had been supported by Egypt under Colonel Gamal Abdel Nasser and the Yemen Arab Republic (YAR), who wanted the new South Yemen to become part of a united homeland. The NLF had broken away from Egypt in 1966, in a move which appears to have given them the upper hand at independence. Very radical, even by Egyptian standards, their general plan was to subsume the "backward" north under the more "progressive" south. They believed that unity could not be achieved until the north "saw the light of socialism". British plans for a Federation of South Arabia were rejected. Since 1905, the entire country of Yemen had been divided, north from south, by a border agreed by the twin colonial powers in the region of the time, the Ottomans and the British.

The leader of the NLF, Qahtan al-Sha'abi, became the new country's first president. All of the PRSY's new leaders were youthful and inexperienced. They had to contend with economic devastation in Aden caused by the loss of business in the port as a result of the Suez Canal having been closed in 1967 following the Six-Day War between Egypt and Israel, as well as the closure of the British base, taking with it jobs and subsidies. Tens of thousands of skilled and educated people left Aden as a result of the British withdrawal. The new country had, at that time, precious little natural resources or agriculture.

Added to these difficulties, the PRSY's new government was susceptible to attacks from across its borders by armed militants belonging to FLOSY, and the NLF leaders were also wary of the powerful South Arabian Army which it had inherited from the Federation.

Within the party, the NLF was divided between Marxist revolutionaries and a more pragmatic socialist wing. In 1968 there was a botched military coup in Aden and a left-wing uprising. A semblance of stability was achieved in June 1969 when the revolutionaries ousted Qahtan al-Sha'abi in a coup, which they called the "Glorious Corrective Move", and started to form a new state, under Salim Rubayya Ali, who had previously been an NLF field commander in the countryside outside Aden.

This period saw the first time ever that the whole of South Arabia had come under one centralised government. However, stability still eluded the fledgling country, since there was precious little infrastructure with which to control the whole of the disparate chiefdoms all the way to the Omani border.

The PRSY became the People's Democratic Republic of Yemen (PDRY) and ever more Marxist in its outlook. Soviet Moscow became attracted by the determination of the new leaders to build this surprising new socialist state and decided to back their experiment, whilst also exploiting strategic opportunities in the region. Not only Soviets, but also personnel from other Communist countries began arriving in Aden. The Soviets helped reform, train and equip the PDRY's armed forces. Yugoslav and Bulgarian pilots finally arrived to fill the vacancies left by Airwork's British ones, who had been expelled in February 1968. East Germany set up a mini Stasi in Aden. Cubans and Chinese also began arriving. Training camps were opened in Aden, and South Yemenis were sent to the countries of the Communist bloc to be educated and trained.

Whilst the PDRY received such assistance, Moscow and its allies failed to invest in the country, finding it easy to make use of the facilities afforded by the South Yemenis without having to do so. The PDRY became a sort of an associate member of the Soviet Bloc and supported Moscow in the Cold War of the time, thus alienating and isolating itself from most of the rest of the world. Mass organisations representing various interest groups of the South Yemeni people were formed, ostensibly to represent them, but in reality to support the government. Party leaders demanded obedience, and in the early years a siege mentality, based on paranoia gave rise to abuses of power, which were labelled by a later president as "the difficult days". Although they tended to hail from the north, and relied on support from their homeland tribes, the PDRY leaders set out to eliminate tribalism. They also eschewed Islam, aiming instead to set up a secular state. Just about everything in Aden, during the first two years after independence when the Balkwill family lived there, was in a state of flux, and there was a lot of fear.

Into this mix moved an assortment of revolutionary organisations, to be hosted by the presiding Marxist regime: the PLO (Palestine Liberation Organisation), and the Red Army Faction also known as the Baader Meinhof group, for instance. I have personally heard of members of these groups living in White City houses that we had only recently vacated. The notorious international terrorist, Carlos the Jackal, lived for a while in Aden at that time.

Later, in October 1977, the world's attention was briefly focused on the airport at Aden. Situated close to the White City, a Lufthansa Boeing 737–230, which had been hijacked by four members of the Popular Front for the Liberation of Palestine (PFLP) in order to secure the release of imprisoned Red Army Faction leaders, landed there. The aircraft had taken off from Palma de Mallorca four days earlier, making stops in Rome, Larnaca, Bahrain and Dubai before Aden. At Aden, the leader of the hijackers executed the captain of the plane as he knelt on the floor of the passenger cabin. The plane refuelled and went on to Mogadishu in Somalia where it was stormed and all the passengers released.

In July 1968, South Yemen Air Force staff were given three months written notice by Airwork of possible termination of their contracts. The letter, however, contained the paragraph:

"If, during the period of notice, the present difficulties are overcome this notice would be withdrawn and your continued employment with this Company in Aden would be assured."

As it happened, Airwork staff and families did remain in Aden well into 1969, when, first, the families left for the UK, followed by the first staff members to leave. Just a handful of the men were left living and working at the Khormaksar airbase when Peter Balkwill, the *Boy from the Moor*, was killed on 21st December 1969.

Chapter Twelve

From Gosport to Khormaksar
(Pamela's Story)

The familiar sight for the Airwork
families in Aden of an aircraft taking
off over Khormaksar airbase.

Born in Gosport, Hampshire during the Second World War, Pamela made her entrance into the world at what was arguably a British front line of that terrible conflict.

Situated at Gosport at the time was the shore establishment of HMS Dolphin, home of the Royal Navy Submarine Service. On the opposite shore, just a one minute boat ride across Portsmouth Harbour, lay the Naval Base itself in the city of Portsmouth. A host of other defence establishments were also concentrated in that tight and densely populated section of the UK south coast, and this made the area a magnet for persistent aerial bombardment by the rival German Luftwaffe, fighting viciously for supremacy.

Growing up under the treacherous skies of wartime Gosport was precarious. Families got by as best they could. Parents and children knew well that each new dawn, casting its early light over their broken and smouldering neighbourhoods, could be the last they might ever wake to. They lived from moment to moment.

For little Pamela, a further childhood challenge came in the form of significant illness. She was hospitalised for much of her young life with serious respiratory problems.

The legacy of the war continued on for years for the citizens of Gosport. Post-war demolition, clearing and relentless construction work remodeled a town whose every street corner, terrace of homes, shop, pub, school and civic place had been well-known, well-worn and even more well-loved through time, up until hostilities had blown the place apart. Against this backdrop of relentless and shifting change, Pamela grew to womanhood. By the time she was in her early twenties she was the mother of three boys and married.

Pamela's husband, like a large proportion of the peers he had grown up with in Gosport, was employed in the defence industry. As such, he worked long periods away, putting strain on the fledgling marriage.

This left Pamela ducking and diving to make life work for her and her boys in the home she and her now absent husband had set up.

All her life Pamela had had to be resilient and a survivor. These were traits that were to stand her in good stead for what would come next.

In 1968, Pamela's husband arranged for the family to join him in Aden, where he was working on a contract with Airwork at South Yemen's air force base at Khormaksar. He and Pamela agreed that this might constitute a fresh start in light of their increasingly difficult marriage.

Boy from the Moor, the story of the search for my missing father, who met his demise in Aden in 1969 whilst working for Airwork at Khormaksar, is based on a blog I published in a series of monthly installments from 2017–2018. In January 2018, I received a message from Pamela. She had discovered my blog online and recognised the Airwork scenario I had described in Aden from her time there with her husband and the characters involved. In fact, she realised that she not only knew who my father was, but also, as a near neighbour of ours in the Khormaksar compound, had known my entire family. Indeed, I had been a school and playmate to her three sons, who were all around the same age as me.

Pamela sent me the photo of the air force compound at Khormaksar, which sits at the header to this chapter.

Pamela and I agreed to meet, and, she, along with her second husband, who had been employed by Airwork, Khormaksar, gave me a comprehensive account of their time in Aden. This both corroborated my childhood memories and gave me fascinating glimpses into their particular experiences, which were as unusual as any of us had in that place. In some instances, they were able to clarify long held questions I had had about the Airwork families' Aden venture and about what might have happened to my father.

Pamela opened the conversation by describing how she came to travel to Aden. Pamela's first husband had originally proposed that she and the boys would fly to Aden in late October 1968. However, Pamela was delayed by a crisis at home, her mother having suffered a serious accident. Eventually though, after she had satisfactorily tended to her mother's needs, Pamela set off with her sons on Friday 13th December 1968. Possibly unlucky for some, but for Pamela it was a date that she would never forget as the beginning of her adventure of a lifetime. She had never before travelled more than 50 miles from her home.

So it was that she set off on the first leg of her journey from Gosport to Khormaksar that wintry UK day via the short ferry hop to Portsmouth. Her three boys, ranging in ages from four to eight years old, were each marked with labels showing their names and travel details. They had between them an array of luggage to transport.

At Portsmouth the young family boarded a train to London. Once in the capital they had to transfer to the air terminal that was, as my own family would have already known it from our travels out to Khartoum and then Aden, still at that time the first point of contact for Heathrow

Airport, and was situated by Victoria Station. Here Pamela met an unexpected challenge. Completely unused to travelling abroad, and not having been advised about this detail, she had failed to obtain visas for Aden. But no matter. Pamela recalls that helpful staff made a series of phone calls, and soon she was told that she was free to travel the next part of her long journey. The intrepid little party then made their way on to Heathrow.

Having never before set foot in an airport, Pamela remembers being astounded at the "large cavern of a place" that Heathrow turned out to be. Although, she commented, it was nothing like as busy then as it is today. She and the boys made their way straight upstairs to the restaurant area. She has no recollection at what point their luggage was taken from them. I suspect that it had been checked in at Victoria whilst she was preoccupied with the visa debacle.

It was then during a brief visit to the WC that Pamela was startled by a disembodied voice announcing, seemingly from the ceiling, the Middle East Airlines flight to Aden. Pamela had never before come across a tannoy system.

Recognising that this was a call for her flight, she rounded the boys up and hurried down a corridor. Here the directionless little family were scooped up by a uniformed person who propelled them direct (Pamela remembers no passport control or security check, also probably as a result of having already checked in at Victoria) from airport building, across tarmac, up aircraft steps to seats at the back of the Aden bound aircraft. These seats, Pamela was authoritatively told, were the aircraft's safest.

As the plane took off Pamela remembers being "excited" yet "scared". Their first transit stop, she recalls, was Beirut. They were allowed to get off the plane and she remembers vividly the impact of the Middle Eastern heat as she stepped into the Lebanese sunshine. After all, it had been bleak mid-winter in London when she had boarded what had come to seem a time and motion capsule that was the aircraft.

By way of further introduction to the Middle East, Pamela saw all around her local people in distinctive and all-encompassing flowing robes of Arabic dress. By contrast she used her time at Beirut airport to change her winter clothes for a fashionable light cotton outfit, of matching blue paisley print top and mini skirt. Her eldest son, meanwhile, had seemingly had an experience of culture difference all of his own: the eight-year-old excitedly told his mother as they re-boarded the plane that he had just seen a man take a cigarette from a fresh packet, light it up, and then throw the packet, still bristling with the remaining cigarettes away. The post-war Britain that he had been growing up in had only recently left behind the austerity of wartime rationing and an overall mentality of thrift was still prevailing. Indeed, Pamela had not forgotten that during her own childhood cigarettes, most especially Woodbines, were usually only bought loose, maybe two or three at a time, owing to the inability of customers to afford a whole packet at once. She and her son were discussing this phenomenon of the wasteful cigarette smoker when an Arab gentleman took her aside and advised her politely that a leg-revealing mini skirt, whilst attractive and fashionable in Western countries, might not be the most conducive form of attire on conservative Middle Eastern streets.

With all the passengers on board and seated, Pamela and her sons ranged once again across the back row, the plane took off for the next transit stop of Jeddah in Saudi Arabia, the last before Aden.

At Jeddah, Pamela remembers, she was offered the opportunity to disembark onto the airfield to stretch her legs, but she was too tired. Her eight-year-old son, however, was keen for the adventure. Besides he had befriended a couple of unaccompanied children on the flight that were going to be getting off and he wanted to join them. Pamela clearly remembers that these children were travelling from boarding school in the UK to join their parents, who lived in the Little Aden area of Aden where the father worked for BP, for Christmas. One of the children was blind. Pamela allowed her son to go.

Once the children had left the plane however, Pamela suddenly panicked that they were unsupervised. But they turned back up again safely, along with a whole new complement of passengers. These were local people, bringing on board a variety of their goods and chattels, including live chickens, the colourful and lively like of which Pamela had never before seen.

The Middle East Airlines jet carrying Pamela and her family finally arrived at their destination of Aden around three o'clock in the morning. She and the boys emerged from the plane into the darkness of a remote part of the airfield and had to walk for some distance across, what they call in that part of the world "the *bondu*" (waste ground), to the airport building to be met by her husband and an Airwork representative. They transferred immediately to her new home nearby. There were no formalities carried out at Khormaksar Airport, only the retrieval of the luggage.

Arriving as she did at her new home in the White City compound in

December, Pamela was astounded at the grand scale of the house, just as my mother had been just a few months previously, in her case, when moving locally from the Dhobi Lines flats into the same White City street. It was quite unlike anything she had ever lived in in the UK. "It was like a palace", she said. "Lots of rooms, all big and all airy. A big bathroom with walk-in shower. Quite unbelievable."

In the morning the family awoke to the unfamiliar and haunting refrain of a muezzin's call to prayer. This sound was emanating, Pamela later found out, from a mosque situated on an army camp immediately behind the house. The sound was to become an everyday feature of her home life in Aden.

Just beyond the side of the house was the airbase. This, of course, was the headquarters of the South Yemen Air Force, to whom her husband had been seconded by his British employer Airwork. Pamela's life was to revolve around this base over the coming year of her life, and be reshaped by events that happened during that time.

Being Pamela's first day in the strange surroundings of her new Aden home, she felt she had no time to waste. So she set immediately about setting the house straight. Then that first evening she went with her husband to the district of Ma'alla where she was astonished to see shops alive with trade, something she had never known at such a late time of day back home in Gosport.

The children had to be taken to school straight away, including her youngest, who at four years old, was starting school for the first time. As had happened with my mother when we arrived in Aden in early 1968, Pamela's children's schooling had already been arranged by Airwork over and above her head before she arrived in the country. And she found herself swept along on the firm's iconic white bus with the rest of us Airwork children from Khormaksar to the school at Steamer Point. She admitted to me that she felt emotional letting go her children at a place that she had not personally agreed or signed up to. In time Pamela was to become yet another name on the rota of mothers that would accompany this bus on its daily school runs through the streets of Aden.

My mother was also on the bus rota, but interestingly, especially as we were near neighbours of hers at the White City compound, Pamela does not remember anything about my mum. Indeed, during our interview, both she and her second husband, Terry, told me they each consider my parents to have been people who "kept to themselves".

Pamela and I shared further memories of the school run: we kids, at the stroke of midday, streaming out, pocket money of a few Adeni fils in hand, excitedly storming the peanut vendor, a local man who strategically located himself at the school gate each day. Many hands grabbing for cones of freshly roasted nuts. Mums, cheerfully head counting amid the melee, herding kids forward, up and onto the big white school bus. Boys and girls crowding the vehicle's humidly hot interior, balancing satchels and water bottles, tuck boxes and books and nut cones. The after-school euphoria subsiding as children flopped here and there, sweaty and sticky, onto squeaky plastic bench seats, settling for their homeward journey.

Recalling these scenes, and remembering her own schooldays in quite another place and time and climate, Pamela described the Airwork daily school bus routine as like "being in another world".

I asked Pamela if she remembered the African driver of the big, white bus, the man that was my father's Sudanese friend. She countered that she thought she remembered him as being Somali. She knew for sure though that he answered to the name of "Sambo", an affectionate nickname that had been coined in the mists of history, long before our time, now seen as racially insensitive, but a sign of those times.

Pamela remembers our driver as being a happy person and very helpful with the children. And she told me her own special story about him: during her time in Aden, Pamela employed a Somali *ayah* named Hanib, who was, Pamela says, very beautiful. She would arrive early for work each morning and Pamela would see her lovely face through the glass pane of the back door, as she sat on the doorstep waiting to be let in. She always wore a beautiful sari. Pamela recalls that she paid Hanib a monthly wage equivalent to seven UK pounds, with which Hanib would buy gold, since paper money was virtually worthless at that time. Hanib was a wonderful house help and all of Pamela's boys have never forgotten her to this day. When it came time for Pamela and the family to leave Aden for good, Hanib begged to be taken with them. With heavy heart, Pamela had had to explain to Hanib that it would be impossible for her to join them. Privately she feared what would become of her. So she was delighted when back in the UK, to later hear from Aden that two of her favourite people that had been left behind, Hanib the *ayah* and "Sambo" the bus driver, had, following the departure of the last Airwork staff, become engaged to be married. She could not think of a more positive outcome for either of them in such difficult circumstances.

An employee rides the iconic Airwork "big white bus".

Like the Balkwills, Pamela's husband had bought a Fiat 500 car. Pamela reminisced to me about finding her freedom in Aden, in large part owing to this little bubble of a car. The Airwork men, her husband included, would start work at around 5.30am to 6am. They were all collected by the big white bus on its first trip of the morning to be taken to the airfield. The bus would then return to pick up the children for the daily school run across Aden. The men would then, once the bus had returned from the school, be brought back home for a breakfast break. In that short time that she had on her own each day between the kids leaving for school and her husband coming home for breakfast, Pamela would hop into the car and drive around discovering the area. She had swiftly obtained her driving licence, she told me, by merely presenting her UK one, along with a photo of herself to the police, who instantly granted her her Aden documents. No driving test required. She particularly liked to pull up at nearby Khormaksar Beach and savour the wild, salty air that whipped across the expanse of surf and sand, lashing her face and blowing her hair and making her glad to be alive. Pamela would be back at the house, car parked up, food on the table, her hair and clothes patted smooth from the beach-side ruffling in time for her husband's return for breakfast. The promptness of this routine was important as, because Pamela was still new in Aden, he was not at all keen on her driving alone and she did not want him to know about her furtive adventures. Eventually however, one breakfast visit, Pamela's husband rumbled her when he discovered that the car engine was unexpectedly hot! He realised instantly that Pamela was the only possible culprit and was not amused.

Pamela's secret car trips in Aden represent to me the resourcefulness and zest for life that she possessed. These were key to her surviving and thriving in the great melting cauldron of difficulties and upheaval that embroiled Aden in its mess during that year of 1968 to 1969. Indeed, although I was young then, I do vaguely recollect Pamela, since she was mum to the boys who lived near me, and she accompanied our school bus. I can still see her younger face now, always smiling.

Pamela's home life lurched forwards through that crazy time in that strange place, much the same as down the street at the Balkwill household, in unpredictable and unforgettable fashion. Whilst she cooked food remarkably similar to supper table fare back in the UK, a stew perhaps, followed by a cake (baked from flour from which weevils would have been carefully sifted) whilst the boys watched TV, there the picture of British family life ended. Rather than throw left over food in the dustbin outside, as in the UK, here scraps had to be buried outside. The oven-like temperature of Aden, combined with haphazard rubbish collection would have resulted in rotting, stinking waste in no time at all. And for the children there was a choice of only two children's programmes (Top Cat and a show about Sir Lancelot, her now fully-grown children remember) to watch on the television at any time ever, unlike the selection from three channels available at home in the UK. Around the house chit chat lizards darted everywhere. Ants, marching in columns, thwarted the "Flit" spray showered on them by an exasperated, aerosol wielding Pamela, to colonise the house. Untended goats marauded outside.

"Those goats got EVERYWHERE in Aden," Pamela said. And she told the story of going to visit a friend in hospital one day and coming across one goat making his way up the stairs towards the wards.

A childhood accident, one day, transcended the local language barrier at Pamela's house. A vegetable vendor, who plied regularly the White City homes of the Airwork families with his produce, called on Pamela as usual. This was just as she was discovering that her eldest son had sliced his big toe whilst playing outside; blood everywhere. The Adeni man immediately abandoned all to gently scoop the boy in his arms and carry him to the kitchen of the house where he tenderly treated the wound. This without a word said between him and the boy or his mother. He spoke no more English than they could talk Arabic. Actions and expressions conveyed all that needed to be said.

Soon Pamela began exercising her independent spirit more widely. Her husband could only be passive to this, since he was at work or otherwise occupied with his own activities. She began to use the family car to explore Aden further. Dodging unpredictable local traffic, such as camels with carts who took so long to negotiate traffic lights that she could have endured at least three cycles from green through red before she could move forward in her car, she took herself on shopping trips to Tawahi. This had, of course, until recently at independence, been the thriving duty-free retail area of the port of Aden at Steamer Point, a well-known shopping mecca throughout the British Empire and, indeed the world. But in this time of post-colonial flux, with Aden sliding into the far reaches of the world's collective memory, Pamela, to her wide-eyed amazement, found only flyblown shopping streets. Here, row upon row of faded and unprepossessing façades, she discovered, fronted shop interiors that were stacked with unimaginably attractive booty, goods from around the world that had, during the port's formerly prosperous times, been stock piled for duty-free sale to visiting ships' passengers. Now, uncalled for and growing stale, being sold off dirt cheap by merchants desperate to close up shop and move on to new and more fertile retail centres around the globe. Pamela wished she could afford some Mikimoto cultured pearls, but even to the slashed prices of these exquisitely beautiful jewels, an Airwork salary would not stretch. Instead she bought a black bikini for wear at the former colonial establishments of the lido at Tarshayn beach or the beachfront Italian Club. Imported from "swinging London" she obtained this trendy swimsuit from Bhicagee Cowasjee, which had been the flagship Indian department store of duty-free Aden. And, at a warehouse that lurked amid the warren of alleyways behind Tawahi's formal crescent of showcase retail outlets, Pamela and the Airwork wives stocked up on dirt-cheap Lancôme products. Representing the mere handful of Western women currently present in Aden, this place, piled high with luxury cosmetics from Europe, was like a private playground for Pamela and these women who, ordinarily, could not possibly have afforded such things.

The Fiat, Pamela said, would again be pressed into service come the afternoons. On hangover-free days (because increasingly wilder parties were being thrown by the Airwork residents of the White City compound the more Aden destabilized around them in that period) she would bundle the children into the little car for a snatched after school trip to swim at Tarshayn or the Italian Club.

A particular adventure that Pamela got caught up in, which occurred at the Italian Club, tells the story of abandoned Aden, and the closing down of Empire in general: she and a girlfriend were sunning themselves by the shoreline at the Italian Club one day when a British man neither of them had seen before pulled up in a speedboat in the shallows nearby. He swam over to the pair and chatted with them. He told them he was in Aden on a special mission. Intriguing as this was to the two women, what seemed even more inviting to them was the chance to see Gold Mohur Beach Club, which lay just along the coast. It was a private club, which neither of them had been to before and this stranger was offering to taken them there in his speedboat. The party set off, roaring across choppy Indian Ocean waves, past a geological feature cast in ubiquitous volcanic rock that so resembled the side of an elephant that the bay that it flanked to one side became known during colonial Aden as "Elephant Bay", the women having been promised prompt delivery back to the Italian Club.

In fits and shouts above sea air that slapped their faces, Pamela and her friend learned during the journey the nature of the stranger's special assignment in Aden: this man was an agent sent (Pamela thinks, possibly by the Royal Mint) from the UK to burn all outstanding money left behind in Aden following the recent British withdrawal.

At withdrawal after withdrawal, during an intense period of the mid 20th century, the British either destroying or removing the various ephemera that had been key to the running of their colonies became a common theme. Whilst the destruction of currency in Aden, it seems from what Pamela has said, came after the withdrawal in 1968, I have already spoken earlier in the book about the heavy lifting of supplies and infrastructure around the actual time of withdrawal from Aden in November 1967. The burning of official colonial papers, however, began as early as 1966. Declassified Foreign Office documents from 2013, that were transferred to the National Archive, reveal an instruction issued in 1961 by the then Colonial Secretary Iain Macleod that independence governments should not be handed any material that "might embarrass Her Majesty's government", that "could embarrass members of the police, military forces, public servants or others, e.g. police informers", that "might betray intelligence sources", or that might "be used unethically by ministers in the successor government". The 50-year-old declassified documents show that diplomatic bonfires were built across the world as a purge known as Operation Legacy was carried out at the handover of each colony. I know that Aden was no exception to this ruling as I personally recall a former Political Officer of the Overseas Civil Service in Aden and its Protectorates describing to me how he spent the last months of British rule in Aden behind the fence of the former married quarters of RAF Khormaksar burning classified files.

Pamela remembers Gold Mohur from her trip there with the unidentified moneyman exactly as I still picture it in my childhood memories. It was the beach club that my family belonged to, and it was a shady oasis of gentility and calm at the very furthest reaches of the haphazard habitation of the peninsula of revolutionary 1968 Aden.

In an action evocative of many mad moments of the Airwork expat experience in Aden, Pamela's charming speedboat host disappeared as soon as they arrived at Gold Mohur. She and her friend were thus obliged to seek out an Airwork neighbour to deliver them home. She arrived back at the White City compound in time to lay the family's table for tea, as though nothing out of the ordinary at all had happened to her that very afternoon.

Having mused on these memories Pamela went on to summarise her emotions. How, newly arrived from Gosport, and by virtue of the little Fiat car and her hastily awarded driving licence, she had been able to set herself free in this distant and complex land. She called Aden a "semi-paradise" saying that, despite deepening revolution and chaos all around, Aden was to her a fascinating and exciting place, the like of which she never dreamed, back in Gosport, that she would end up in. She described how she lived her life against an exotic, feudal backdrop. Intensely hot and barren, an Arabic-speaking world of traditional customs and dress where she was able to speak her own language, and wear clothes she was accustomed to (contrary to what she had been politely advised by the Arabic gentleman passenger on her incoming aircraft journey, she came to find that miniskirts were acceptable attire in Aden after all). Despite Islamic tradition, she was able to drink alcohol should she choose. Pamela told me that she was, in fact, bamboozled by the drinking culture, having been used to just having the odd glass of sherry back home in Gosport, suddenly being liberally served glasses of measureless rums and cokes, gin and Merrydown cider at expat parties. And, as a woman, she was free to take advantage of all the adventure that Aden held. Moving between the four remaining centres containing British citizens left in Aden — Airwork, the BP refinery, Cable and Wireless and the British Embassy — she made friends from all walks of British life. Although, she said, along with a very small contingent of American marines, based near the Rock Hotel at Steamer Point, Airwork was the liveliest. Boredom in this abandoned, far-flung place might have been a possibility for some, of course, but not for the resourceful Pamela. Talk turned to Pamela's boys, and us Airwork children in general, in Aden.

Pamela said that she felt that their new life in Aden came as something of a "wake up call" for her young sons. In particular when they saw how local children went about their lives in the streets around them. Some had been wounded as a result of the hostilities that had taken place up to the recent independence. Others had to beg for a living. Many beggars were disabled, such as one boy with damaged legs who had to move himself about on a trolley. Another boy, to whom Pamela regularly donated money when she would pass him at the local Khormaksar shops, had only one leg and walked with a cane. But, Pamela noted, he possessed integrity. The odd evenings that she and her family would visit the Shanaz Cinema nearby, she would come across this one-legged boy beggar there. However, he would never ask her for money on those occasions, knowing that he had already had his fair share of contributions from her elsewhere. Pamela was saddened to learn that some child beggars had been deliberately maimed by adults in order to bring income to their families.

And she compared her sons' childhood existence in the White City compound as being like a "whole new world". Trustful, and following the example of childhood back in the UK, and in common with other Airwork mothers, Pamela would allow them out to play in the streets of the compound.

The boys relished this freedom of course. They would meet up with other Airwork children, such as myself. They would take themselves off to the perimeter gate to a kiosk where they could buy pocket money treats. All of us kids owned gaily-decorated school satchels that were bought from this place. Pamela realised our gang of kids would get ourselves into a certain amount of mischief, which we did, but it was an innocent fun kind of mischief.

However, nobody was prepared for what was about to happen: sometime in mid-1969, all the Airwork parents learned in a meeting, that was hastily called by the company's operations manager, that certain children had been subjected to abuse by strangers.

As a result, restrictions on access for women and children on camp were announced. Pamela said that no more information of any substance was given, and she was bemused by the whole incident.

However, Airwork took the matter so seriously that it was not long before the families were sent back to the UK, and from thereon, all foreign postings were listed as unaccompanied.

Pamela had another matter on her mind by this time however, and back in the UK she quickly forgot the child abuse scandal in Aden. In Khormaksar she had met and fallen in love with Terry, and she was now waiting for him to return to be with her.

Terry — who had embarked on his two-year contract at Khormaksar with visions of buying a brand new Rover 2000 with leather seats (he had already acquired a sample book before leaving the UK) with enhanced earnings, did indeed return to Pamela. Meeting her had proved a life-changing course for him in Aden. Instead of the Rover 2000 with leather seats, he ended up back in the UK with a Ford Cortina Mark I with a sloppy gear shift, a house and three young boys. The couple married in 1971.

Gradually all the men came back, and most went on to other Airwork contracts around the Middle East. Terry went, unaccompanied by his new wife Pamela, as per Airwork's new directive, to Abu Dhabi to work for a while before coming home to family life with her and the boys on the south coast of the UK, where they still live today.

And it was not long after the families left that all the Airwork men began arriving back in the UK. Following an ultra left-wing coup in June 1969, young firebrand politicians of the new Government, former anti-British revolutionaries of Aden's colonial era, decreed it inappropriate that the new country's air force should be staffed by British employees. Replacement personnel had been brought in from Communist countries and the Airwork contract had been terminated.

My father also had been contracted to join the Airwork Abu Dhabi operation. However, as one of the last employees left on the ground in Aden at Christmas 1969 he was unexpectedly killed, and so, as we know, never returned from Aden.

It was very interesting for me to hear Pamela's memories of Aden and to compare them to mine and my own family's experience. However, hearing from her about the child abuse in the White City was a stark revelation, and it struck a chord, providing a possible explanation for mysterious events that I had personally experienced in my childhood in Aden and had wondered about for so long: gifts and invitations brought to me at my house by the children that were known to have been involved in the abuse, and which had been instantly rejected by my parents, much to my confused consternation, like the ice cream that my father confiscated and dissected, for instance. Another example was seven-year-old me being taken to the house of the Airwork Operations Manager and, as I nervously sat at his impressive wood dining table, chewing on the straw of a Coca Cola drink that had been served to me there by his house boy, being grilled about who with and where and when I had been playing of late.

Then recently in London, I heard of an Adeni man who claimed that during "Marxist times", girls were being snatched in Aden and sent to camps upcountry for what he termed "technical training". The upshot of this "training" he said was that the girls always got pregnant. Families were sending their girls away from Aden, he claimed, to avoid being snatched for "training". His strange story seems somehow to have corroborated what Pamela told me about child sex abuse at the White City as well as some of my own memories from my childhood there.

Terry joined Pamela's and my conversation. Having joined Airwork straight after leaving the Fleet Air Arm in the UK, he told me he began his career with them at Hurn Airport near Bournemouth. This was a contract that was to begin in the UK and then take him out to the Khormaksar airbase at Aden. He was to be paid four times the salary as a civilian aircraft engineer than he had been receiving in the Navy.

At Hurn, Terry was a part of a group of six men working on first the modifications to six brand new Beaver aircraft that had been bought from Canada. They then stripped the planes down to be air freighted by the RAF out to Aden as part of the air force being set up by the British at Khormaksar, to serve what was going to be the new country of South Yemen after independence from Britain. Terry and the other Airwork guys then flew to Khormaksar themselves to reassemble the Beavers at their new base, and to begin their Airwork contracts in Aden. They arrived at the end of October 1967 within a month of independence.

And so Terry became a colleague of my dad in Aden, although, he told me, he worked in the maintenance division of the operation where my father was employed in administration. At 27 years old he was also a good 18 years my father's junior, and at the time a bachelor, which meant that the two men did not socialise together.

Terry was not able to tell me much about my father other than that he was a reasonably private man, who did not spend much time with the other Airwork men at the mess bar. Interestingly, when I told Terry that my father had been a fluent Arabic speaker, he was shocked. In common with other former Airwork colleagues in Khormaksar, he had never heard my dad speak Arabic in Aden.

What Terry does remember, however, is the time of the withdrawal operation from Aden. Just one of a handful of British nationals who remained on the ground as all British personnel left the colony, this puts him in the unusual position of being one of the last British men alive today who experienced that chaotic event. As well as being a witness to almost the last handover of a colony at the historic close of the British Empire.

In addition, along with my father, he spent that period both working and living at Khormaksar airfield. It was from there that weeks of evacuation of British personnel took place, leading up to the 30th November 1967 departure of Governor Sir Humphrey Trevelyan, whisked away by helicopter, after winding up a British rule of Aden and its hinterland of 128 years. So, Terry's memories provide an important record of that historic event, as well as an interesting insight for me into my father's actual experience. Until I met Terry, I had been relying on my mother's second-hand account of my dad's observations of that unique event.

I asked Terry to tell me about that period.

He spoke about witnessing heavy items that could not be removed from Aden being lifted by helicopter and taken out and dropped at sea. He remembers that, on the final day of evacuation, British troops were driving to the airport to catch flights out, parking up at the roadside and throwing their car keys over the fence into the airfield where the Airwork guys were. Then, once the evacuation was over, he saw the keys being collected, the cars retrieved and then being stored in a hangar. Not long afterwards, he said, the Yemen Army came and took all the vehicles. There were a lot of Mini Mokes and Land Rovers in the haul.

Just before the final evacuation, the Airwork men moved from where they were living in officers' houses in the White City to the comparative safety of the officers' quarters, behind the high fences of the camp. Although Terry spent the day and night of the handover ceremony by Sir Humphrey to the incoming South Yemenis on the camp, he did not witness the event.

Once everyone had gone, the Airwork men were free to roam around what had been the lower ranks' quarters, which looked eerily still occupied. All kinds of belongings had been left behind: sports equipment, clothes and personal belongings and so on. In the Sergeants' mess they found bulk freezers full of food, and many cases of fruit juice and squash. The men continued to roam around helping themselves to these things to make their own quarters comfortable. Until, that is, they were stopped by the Yemeni Army. The NAAFI meanwhile had a big stock of alcohol, and held a closing down sale. The alcohol was so cheap they were virtually giving it away. The Airwork guys had to make a decision whether to fill their trolleys with these knock-down bargains or not, because they didn't know at that time what was to happen to them, whether they would end up staying or leaving. In the end most bought enough booze to last for ages, which turned out to be the right choice, because they ended up remaining for as long as two years.

Those final days of 1967 constituted a period of great uncertainty for the Airwork men. Leading up to the British withdrawal, Airwork's men would be accompanied when walking outside of their air force compound by British army soldiers, for their safety. After the withdrawal they were left existing in a place that was dangerously hostile towards their countrymen, no longer with protection, or with representation by their own Government. The local political climate was so febrile that nobody knew quite what was going to become of the Airwork contract.

Terry recalls an evacuation drill being put in place, whereby Airwork staff, following an alert from a radio technician at the airfield, would be transported from camp to the shore to be whisked away from the trouble in Aden by ship. In the event however, the drill was put into practice only once, later on, after the families had arrived to live at the Khormaksar base. This was the aforementioned occasion that I experienced, which ended up a damp squib when the group of families, under Airwork escort, were, for reasons unclear, turned back at the beach.

Airwork personnel felt comforted to know that their safety was a serious consideration. Terry also said that he had been issued with a revolver for protection. He left this firearm, along with six rounds of ammunition, buried in the ground outside his quarters when he finally left Aden.

With the wives and children not yet in Aden in the uncertain period from the withdrawal into early 1968, the Airwork men lived a sort of a ghost of a life, mostly confined to camp with only each other for company and not much contact with the outside world. Terry described these days as being mixed: some were good days, some boring. Working from seven in the morning to one in the afternoon, the remaining hours of their days seemed very long. Terry looked forward to those occasional afternoons whose monotony was broken by a game or two of squash with his boss and friend, Ray. He and Ray had come together to Khormaksar from Hurn, along with the Beavers. After their squash game the two of them would take tea together, served at their quarters by a houseboy. As these days ran into weeks and then on into a month, Terry and Ray could see, as they relaxed on the terrace of the South Yemen Air Force accommodation, that everything was deteriorating around them. Along with the sudden abandonment by the RAF of their one time flagship airbase, so went their careful maintenance of it. And, as if to magnify the scale of this absence of upkeep, Morning Glory, an invasive creeper, had lately somehow sprung from thick roots that had become entrenched in the sparse volcanic earth, and was now snaking its way unchecked across this corner of camp. At each tea time they saw that the creeper had advanced ever more, choking balustrades, blanketing roofs and oozing through windows and doors.

Terry's houseboy poses outside his quarters at an officers' mess covered in Morning Glory.

Sundown over the Khormaksar camp invariably found Terry, Ray and their Airwork colleagues at the mess bar, where, oftentimes, frustrated by the torpor of their isolated existence, they resorted to daft pranks and games: racing over upturned armchairs, games of tiddly winks and, of course, drinking contests.

Some older guys who were stalwarts of expatriate living, having spent entire careers, spanning back to the earlier part of the 20th century, in the countries of the British Empire, drank heavily. Nearing retirement, and avoiding repatriation to a cold mother country that they barely knew, they now had little else to do but band together in the bar, or around well stocked drinks fridges in their quarters.

From this period until the end of the contract two years later, the single Airwork men continued to live on camp, never returning to the white houses that they had initially occupied when they had arrived in Aden. From early 1968 the families of the married men began to arrive, living first at the Dhobi Lines flats and then at the White City on the airfield's other side.

Following the arrival of the Airwork families in Aden, the Soviets began to come. The first of an influx of nationals from Communist countries from around the world, invited by the new ideological left-wing government of Aden to assist in the setting up of the new South Yemen, which they envisaged as the first Marxist Arab state to ever be created.

Terry talked about the arrival of the Soviet personnel at the airfield. At first these men were kept apart from the British staff, but as their regime's influence in Aden expanded, so the confidence of their workers grew. Before long the Soviet ground engineers were encroaching on the Airwork guys' space at the airfield, increasingly appropriating their tools and equipment. At some point in 1969, Terry remembers a Russian transport aircraft arrived. He and the Airwork men watched as parts of a number of MiG–15 planes were unloaded from the plane and then reassembled.

In February 1968 the British pilots, originally recruited to fly the SYAF planes, had been sacked and sent home, victims of a skirmish between local politicians and Airwork. Terry estimates that seven months went by before their replacements were found. This was a very boring time of inactivity at the airfield. Eventually though, new recruits began to arrive. These were Yemeni cadets and Eastern bloc pilots, whose abilities and standards fell far short of the banished RAF-trained men. Terry particularly remembers an attempted landing on an upcountry desert runway at a time he was flying with a Yugoslav pilot. It is the nearest he has ever felt to death in his life, he said. The pilot ran out of runway and landed up in the sand in spectacular fashion.

One particularly dashing and rascally Yugoslav pilot came to make a name for himself at the SYAF. He lived in a house amongst Airwork staff in the White City. Coming from an Eastern Bloc country that, having liberated itself from Soviet dominance, eschewed Western influence also, this man's ethnicity seemed to fit neatly with his British counterparts amid Marxist Aden. However, he was also a one-off maverick. He partied and drank to excess in the compound, and embarked on a flagrant affair with the wife of a colleague/neighbour. His exploits whilst flying around the great wild open of "upcountry" South Yemen became the stuff of legend back at the Khormaksar camp.

The Yemeni cadets, meanwhile, were not qualified to fly solo and needed assistance. They caused multiple accidents whilst flying upcountry, usually in Beihan, on the border with the Yemen Arab Republic (YAR).

1) View from the air force camp in upcountry Beihan. 2) Salvaging a crashed Beaver plane in Beihan.

Until 1962 the YAR had been referred to as North Yemen and was a feudal kingdom, which had been ruled over by a succession of Mutawak-kilite Imams since 1918. On four or five occasions, Terry and colleagues were obliged to travel up to this far flung spot, delivering supplies, ferrying casualties back to Aden, or to repair or salvage the cadets' damaged planes. Today he remembers those trips to Beihan as being like journeys into a medieval land that time and progress had forgotten.

On one of these sorties, Terry reflected with faint amusement, he and his engineer colleagues came across an Iraqi doctor, working in one of the primitive villages of that remote area. This man could speak English and was very pleasant and the guys enjoyed settling down to chat with him.

Befriending a Soviet-trained Iraqi doctor in upcountry South Yemen.

The Iraqi doctor told them that he had received his medical training in Communist Russia. As part of that scheme he had been sent to perform medical duties in this far-flung spot. The men then got around to discussing international affairs. Being summer of 1969, when the USA had just put the first man on the moon, talk quickly turned to that event. Terry and his colleagues were then astonished when this intelligent medical man refused to acknowledge that the Americans had achieved such a success. He had been indoctrinated such, it seemed, by his Russian benefactors that he believed that only the Soviet Union could be capable of such a feat.

As the interview began to draw to a close Terry and Pamela began to reminisce. They talked of the romance they found with each other in Aden and fun times that they each enjoyed there, despite the surrounding hostilities. Unlike my mother, both of them had positive experiences there. We can only conclude that they had each arrived in Aden from very different backgrounds to Mum. Unlike them, she spent a wartime childhood growing up in a peaceful enclave of the UK (the outskirts of Cambridge) and so did not have the early introduction to the hostility and violence of war that Pamela had had in bomb torn Gosport. And she had gone on to spend her first days as an expatriate in the calm and dignified surroundings of early post-colonial, civilian Khartoum, where Pamela, by contrast, had been pitched straight into revolutionary Aden. Mum had not been quite prepared for the mayhem of post-independence Aden and the harshness of life on a military camp. Whether she was also challenged because she knew that my father was, at that time, in the kind of bind that would soon lead to his death/disappearance is a conjecture.

Pamela talked about the surprise of discovering my *Boy from the Moor* blog online. Having googled "Airwork 1967–1969", she was amazed to find a story with its roots in Aden come up, whose setting was very familiar to her. Characters in photos in the blog were people she knew. She remembered my dad, the eponymous *Boy from the Moor*. She even recognised her own husband, Terry, in one photo.

"It is unbelievable that we are together today," she told me. "I clearly remember you as a little girl, when you would play with my boys." Talk then turned to the most pressing part of my blog: my investigation into the life and death of my father. Both Pamela and Terry expressed surprise at almost all of the facts that I had published that are known about the case:

That my father had been killed after being knocked down by a car. Pamela said that she had been told by her ex-husband — a comment made in passing several months after the event — that he had been hit whilst riding a bicycle.

That his funeral was carried out almost immediately with, according to a letter received by my mother from Airwork, a large congregation present. Both Pamela and Terry thought that little time was given for an investigation into the death, and found it hard to believe that there were enough people left in Aden at that difficult time to form a congregation of any size.

That his effects were not returned in the official trunk that had been afforded all of the returning Airwork staff. My father's belongings were apparently personally delivered to my mother in a holdall bag.

The mystery that my dad, the fluent Arabic speaker, who had talked freely in the language throughout his former life in Khartoum, was not known by anyone in Aden to have uttered a word in the language.

Terry could not remember how he had been told about Peter Balkwill's demise in Aden. And both Terry and Pamela expressed disturbed surprise that they had not understood at the time the mysterious nature of the accident. They were sad for the disillusionment and grief this had brought to my family.

Terry ended the interview with a wry observation: having learnt that my father had allegedly been hit by a car outside the Cold Storage building on the Ma'lla Straight, he explained to me that, during the emergency period that marked Britain's final months before withdrawing from Aden, the bodies of people killed in terror incidents were taken to the Cold Storage building, by way of a temporary morgue... so a strangely fitting backdrop for my father's subsequent fatal accident.

It was an honour and a pleasure for me to visit Pamela and Terry. To hear more about the particular place and time that was Aden in its revolutionary period following independence from Empire. To validate hazy childhood memories of mine. And to hear more about my dad, even if, once again, answers either about his death or life, could not be found.

Boy from the Moor

Chapter Thirteen

Back to the Moor: A Recap and Epilogue

On a family visit back to his
Devonshire homeland, Dad and
I pose to be photographed on
Hatherleigh Moor. Circa 1963.

Back to the Moor

As recounted in earlier chapters, Peter John Balkwill, the *Boy from the Moor*, was born and raised to the age of 16 in Hatherleigh, a market town noted then for farming and for livestock auctions, situated in moorland above Dartmoor in north Devon.

Although I have never actually lived in the hometown of my paternal ancestors, I know Hatherleigh to be a charming and engaging little town, which has been drawing me back since I was a child.

Of course, during the early years before his death in 1969 when I was eight, it would be my father taking us on visits to his Devonshire homeland that first introduced me to Hatherleigh.

In particular, my dad's boyhood love of the moorland that surrounds his hometown is already well known in this story. As a child he would head out for solitary adventures in the wide-open space there. There are some who knew him that have speculated to me that he sought this kind of freedom as an escape from a repressive home life back in town. Certainly my mother talked about him taking her out to the moor in order to drink cider where they might not be seen, as his extended family would frown upon their young relative drinking alcohol. It has also been suggested to me that it was his identifying wide open and far flung places with his need for freedom and self expression that drove my dad to seek a new life for himself in the distant and little-populated lands of the Middle East.

On our family visits to Devon we would go to Exeter first to see his parents, Sam and Margaret, who had relocated there. Then we would head north to the moor and Hatherleigh. There we visited his ageing relatives, not least Olive, who eventually became the last surviving Balkwill to live in the original family home, dying as late as 1992. And it was she who I would travel to Hatherleigh to interview in 1989, kicking off my quest to find out the truth about my missing father; a search which has resulted in the publication of first, my *Boy from the Moor* blog, and now this book.

Despite dutifully returning regularly with us to Hatherleigh, my dad had a love/hate relationship with his hometown and his relatives there. A combination of his antipathy towards the way of life of the town, his schoolboy love of the big, wide world of aviation, and a wanderlust that I think had been instilled in him by his mother Margaret (who had lived in South Africa as a child where, she once told me, she had experienced the Siege of Mafeking), were what had caused him to leave Hatherleigh as early as the age of 16 in 1942.

Later, following Dad's death, my mum Joan took us occasionally to visit her Devon in-laws, during which times they would look us over, their Peter's fatherless children, with curiosity. I could barely understand their Devonshire drawl then as my brother and I had become very much a part of our mother's family, who lived in the east of England, in Cambridge, where accents were completely different. But nevertheless, I was fascinated at each return visit as I realised the importance of the legacy of these people to me, and this place, that had been special to my father, who I had lost too soon.

Returning back to Olive's house from a moorland walk with our mother. My brother and I in Hatherleigh in 1970.

As before said, I interviewed Great Aunt Olive in Hatherleigh in 1989. At that time, I walked the moor and the town's streets and I sat in Olive's time warp front room that my father had once frequented, and which I had sat in on family visits when a child. I marvelled, at that time, at the personal legacy that all these surroundings held for me. Then years later, in 2017, my daughter and I made an emotional trip to the moorland town together, partly as research for this book, but also to introduce her to a slice of what is her heritage too.

Church of St John the Baptist, Hatherleigh.

On that 2017 visit we stood in the road in front of the original Balkwill family house where I had once interviewed Olive. Long since sold, we could only take a look from the outside.

We went on to visit the nearby 15th century church of St John the Baptist. Its graveyard is familiar to me as the resting place of many Balkwill relatives, and as home to the town's war memorial, seen in the photo opposite standing beyond the lychgate, just in front of the church. This memorial commemorates, in particular, the deaths of many, many of one generation of men during World War I. Whilst my grandfather, Sam, and his brother John had returned from the Great War, the Balkwill family destiny was badly impacted by this one tragic event. Most of Peter's many female relatives lost their partners in that war and so remained spinsters for the rest of their lives or married late, thus producing barely any children in Peter's generation of the family. Their collective bitterness at this tragedy, and inability to contain it, was to impact on my father the whole of his life.

Passing through the town square en route to the church, we caught sight of a new addition to the town: a sign that declared "War Horse Country". This was a confirmation to me. Having been to see the eponymous and well-regarded War Horse show in London a while before, I had sat in the audience, watching the plot unfold on the stage in front of me, just knowing from experience that the setting and the storyline must be Hatherleigh, and that of the real life Hatherleigh experience: a generation of men from a small Devon town with a livestock market, heading to the First World War with their horses. Just as Sam, my father's father would have done over 100 years ago. The show is a fantastic illustration, both of the story of those men of Hatherleigh who went to war, and of the town of Hatherleigh at that time.

We visited my father's former home in Moor View and were invited in by Don, the current owner. We saw the primary school my father attended. And briefly we stepped out on the moor just to sample the wildness and openness my father had loved as a boy. With no more Balkwill relatives left in Hatherleigh, this could well have been our last visit to the homeland of Peter, the *Boy from the Moor*.

Recap

Here I will set out to recap *Boy from the Moor*, the story of the life and mysterious death/disappearance of Peter John Balkwill, who was born in Hatherleigh in 1926. An epilogue at the close of the chapter will comment on the progress since the blog that preceded this book was published, and will attempt to rationalise all the information available before concluding, best as I can, the strange, sad tale of Peter Balkwill.

As a reminder of the main premise of the book, which is Peter's death/disappearance in Aden on 21st December 1969, here again is set out the letter, sent to my mother informing her of her husband's death, which is first published in Chapter One:

Death

I was eight years old when two men from Airwork, a company then based at Hurn Airport, Bournemouth, who had employed my aircraft fitter father and sent to him to work for the South Yemen Air Force in Aden, came to our house in Cambridge on 22nd December 1969. They had come to inform us that Dad had been killed in Aden, in the manner that the letter states, on the preceding day.

It was Christmastime, the house was decorated and there were presents under the tree, including some left for us by my dad, who had been with us in the UK a couple of months beforehand, but had returned to Aden alone to finish off his contract there. He would have returned to us early in 1970, then gone off to Abu Dhabi to work on an unaccompanied job, also with Airwork, had he survived.

My mother, apparently, had not wanted to tell us kids about the death immediately, so that we might enjoy Christmas, but I caught her crying that night so she caved in and told me right away. The reason she gave for the death was as the letter states: it was a hit and run accident. But she did a strange thing then, and told me not to discuss it with anybody, a request that I obeyed for many years.

We had lived in Aden with my dad for the two years previous. I had seen many things there that were unusual for a child to witness. The way my mother informed me of his accidental death in 1969, even to an eight-year-old child, seemed disingenuous based on what I knew then of Aden and of my dad. He was then, by all accounts, buried in Aden. No family attended. I grew up not talking about him or his death, but always thinking about it and filled with doubt.

Meanwhile, South Yemen, where Aden is located, was becoming a country more and more closed to an ordinary British person such as myself. Aden had been a British colony up until 1967 at which point the British withdrew and handed over power to a left-wing local government. The Balkwill family were in residence there for two years from this time. But there was unrest amongst the government's predominately youthful and idealistic ranks. There was an attempted coup in 1968, followed by a successful one in 1969, which became known as 'the Glorious Corrective Move'. South Yemen became the only Marxist country ever to have existed in Arabia. From that moment the various Communist and Socialist governments from around the world began to fill Aden with their qualified personnel from all walks of life: military, police, education, health, shipping, agricultural and fisheries and so on. This was ostensibly to aid the ailing, fledgling country. The new South Yemen had not received nearly as good a financial package from the departing British as it should have done in order to keep what had been its flourishing port city of Aden alive in the style to which it was accustomed and its territories fully functioning. These Communist regimes also had the caveat, however, that they would use the globally strategic territory for their own ends. This was the height of the Cold War after all. Additionally, Aden also became home to international terrorist groups and terror training camps.

Revisit

Thus, I was unable to even think of visiting Aden as an independent British traveller. Nor, despite the fact that the place had been a British colony for over a century up until 1967, did I ever meet a fellow Brit who had been there post our 1969 departure who I could ask about it. It was simply a closed place. However, in 1996 I got an opportunity to join a Royal British Legion pilgrimage to visit the two principal graveyards in Aden. This was to honour fallen British servicemen and family members who had died during conflict for the liberation of Aden from the British in its final days as a colony in the 1960s.

This window of opportunity to visit what had become a relatively stable Aden, had come about primarily as a result of the fall of the Iron Curtain in Europe and the ending of the Cold War globally. Communist and Socialist powers that had been residing in, and making use of, Aden during the previous 20 years had now abandoned the territory for their own political-ly emerging countries. In the remaining vacuum, South Yemen and North Yemen had merged in 1990 under President Ali Abdullah Salih. A move which had been imagined for some time and had now finally taken place, providing an uneasy truce which the RBL took advantage of to conduct their first ever pilgrimage to Aden. Fundamental disagreements between north and south endure to this day and, seemingly, will do so for many years to come, causing war, famine, disease and serious privations of all kinds in the "unified" country.

I had been alerted to the pilgrimage by Jack, my father's former line manager with Airwork at the South Yemen Air Force in Aden. He had been introduced to me as a result of my having contacted the former Airwork HQ at Hurn in 1996. By this time, as an adult in my thirties, I had resolved to solve the mystery of what had happened to my dad over 20 years before, and Airwork, followed by Jack, had been my first port of call.

Jack and I had had a big conversation about Aden and about my search for my dad. Jack had told me that he had left Aden already by the time my dad was killed and so could not give me definitive information. But he was interested in the story and he did go so far as to wonder whether an explanation of a hit and run accident, which noted that my father had sustained a head injury that killed him, might have been a cover for some other type of death which had been caused by murder.

Anyway, when I got home from visiting Jack, I contacted the Royal British Legion. Even though my father had not been military, meaning I did not technically qualify to join the trip, they agreed to take me along. I was ecstatic. My first chance to revisit Aden after so many years of wondering, and with all the technical, emotional and knowledgeable back up I could hope for from the RBL.

With the Royal British Legion pilgrimage, November 1996.

We set off for Aden on 25th November 1996. I then returned twice more, in 1997 and 1998 as related in Chapter Three. This was during a quiet time, and before the political situation in Yemen began to change, making the country impossible again to visit, as it is again at the current time of writing.

During the three trips I made to Aden, I was never able to either find the site of my father's grave, or to learn any more about the circumstances in which he died. Significant events DID occur however, but the upshot to them would always be negativity, as follows:

• British Embassy staff working in Aden at the time of my dad's death, or their spouses, where the staff member had died, were contacted and asked what they knew about the death and/or funeral. Strangely for diplomatic circles, and within the small expat community of Aden at that time (1967), nobody knew about either.

• The Aden Consulate records were searched for an entry of his death, but none was found. Eventually a record of it turned up in the Embassy in Sana'a, by then capital of unified Yemen, but the archivist who had made the entry was long since dead, so I could not seek clarification there.

• An article was placed in the local newspaper, Al Ayyam, about my dad's story, asking people to come forward with any information they might have. Nobody did.

• It was established that there were no archives left in any institution in Aden (newspaper/police/court etc) that could be consulted for information. All had been lost during civil war and strife that had occurred during the intervening 20 years.

• Through contacts, the Adeni man who had lived next door to us when I was a child in Aden was found. I spoke to him on the phone from my hotel, but the conversation was bewildering. Whilst he confirmed some aspects of my father's case, as I have always known it, other facts did not tally. For instance, he was adamant that the hit and run story was true. He said that my father had been crossing the dual carriageway at Ma'alla to a waiting taxi, having completed his purchases at the Cold Store shop that he had been visiting. He went on to make the stunning revelation that my father had misjudged oncoming traffic because he was drunk. The waiting taxi and the drunkenness were completely new facts to me, never having been mentioned in despatches by his employers, Airwork, at the time of the death. This man made two other assertions:

1) He confirmed a barely believable statement that my mother had once made: that the driver of the car that had hit my father was being driven by a

resident of the White City (situated some 10 miles or so from the site of the accident at Ma'alla), who was also a colleague at the South Yemen Air Force, a trainee Yemeni pilot. He put a possible name to the young pilot, but told me that the man was now dead.

2) He stated that the reason I could not find my father's grave in Ma'alla Christian Cemetery, or anywhere else in Aden, was that he had actually been cremated very soon after his death. That information goes against everything that was reported to us in the UK by Airwork at the time. Foreign Office and other professional personnel who knew Aden well commented that it was barely believable that a cremation would have taken place in 1969, as there were no facilities there at that time to do so. The remaining Hindu population that had not left Aden at independence were duly contacted to find out if they might have conducted such an operation, in keeping with their faith, but they confirmed that they were certain that no such cremation of anybody had been undertaken at that time. My former next door neighbour, a charming man, both as I remembered him from when I was a child in 1968–69 and then as I came to know him from phone conversations in 1997, was subsequently dismissed as being, with all that he had told me on the phone, a red herring in the story of the disappearance of my father, a man he claimed to have remembered fondly.

• Ali Nadir, an Adeni-born, former British Army officer took me out for the day to Holkat Bay Cemetery, an old, Victorian British cemetery, where we paced the area to see if we might miraculously find a head stone for my father there. We could not. Nadir had already checked both Ma'alla Christian Cemetery where my dad was supposed to have been buried, as well as the British military cemetery at Silent Valley, on behalf of the British Legion before I had arrived in Aden. To no avail.

Planting a cross at Ma'alla Christian Cemetery in remembrance of my father.

A single positive and heart-warming development during the trip was that Gerry, the pilgrimage leader, produced a cross, made of oak, that he had commissioned with my father's name and details on. He asked me to choose an unmarked grave within Ma'alla Christian Cemetery to make my dad's own, and a private service was held there with the cross being dedicated to my father.

Back Home

In the next two or three years or so following the three Aden trips, I spent time following up leads, tying up loose ends from earlier parts of my life, and making last ditch appeals for anyone who might have known my father. I wanted to do everything I could before putting what had become an emotionally and physically exhausting search on the back burner. Of course, it will never be entirely shelved as new information could always arise at any moment that may lead to the ultimate conclusion that has always been desired.

• I set out to trace the Reverend Ian Findlay, who is mentioned in the Airwork letter to my mother shown earlier in the chapter, as the minister who conducted my father's burial service. I had found out whilst in Aden that this man had been a minister of The Church of Scotland. I contacted the church, only to be told that Reverend Findlay had died years before. Apparently he had been attached to the Church of Scotland's ministry that was based out of Bombay at the time, and no records remained from that period and place.

• I also set out to trace the photographs and tape recording of the ceremony that are referred to in the same letter. My mother told me that she had placed them with her solicitor for safekeeping. I contacted his office. He had retired long before, but they gave me his home number and he agreed to talk to me. We had a long phone chat. He remembered the case well, but he also remembered that my mother had never given him any photos or a tape recording. Somewhere along the line truth had become distorted.

• I turned my attention to the death certificate, also mentioned in the letter. This is when I remembered that my stepfather had been shocked to learn that, when he was due to marry my mother some 15 years earlier, she could not produce the required death certificate of her first husband. He had had to apply to Aden as a result of that for a copy certificate, no mean feat in 1983 when South Yemen was still deeply Communist and a closed country. The copy certificate he obtained is shown below.

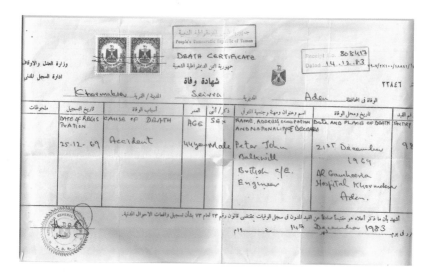

• I tracked down our former UK neighbour, who had been involved in helping us out on the night that the Airwork representatives had travelled from their base in Bournemouth to Cambridge to inform us of the death. She had since moved to Ireland, and when I finally found her and spoke to her on the phone she was on holiday in Sri Lanka. This lady told me that she had been telephoned during the day of the night in question (22nd December 1969) by Airwork to ask if she would assist them in the task of informing my mother. A friend and colleague of my dad's in Aden, who had at times visited us in Cambridge during his home leave, had given the UK head office her details. The two men involved then called at her house once they arrived in Cambridge. She and one of her sons had then come over to our house to collect my brother and me to take us to their place for the duration. She remembers entering by the back door into the kitchen where my mother was ironing. It was early evening and they then came into the living room where my brother and I were watching television and scooped us up to take to their house. The Airwork gentlemen were then able to talk to my mother alone. We kids were then returned home later in the evening. My former neighbour also remembers a few weeks later, after Christmas, that my mother made a bonfire in the back garden and burned my father's effects. She remarked that many of the aspects of the case of my father's death were strange: the bonfire (she speculated that Mum might have been destroying incriminating evidence relating to Dad), the manner in which we were informed, the fact that my mother did not attend the funeral in Aden, and that his body was not brought home. We also discussed that it was odd that my mother had told me that I was not to discuss openly my father's death.

• Via an aircraft forum where I appealed for anyone who might have known my father, I received two responses, each of them from men that knew my dad well, in both Sudan and Aden, and who I personally remember from my childhood. It was with great sadness that the Aden colleague learned of the trials my family have been through with the nature of my dad's death. He is yet another person who was not in Aden at the time of the accident, and had had no idea of the full extent of the true circumstances.

• In south Devon, I tracked down John Warren, my father's best friend from school days in Hatherleigh. John had done his national service with my dad in Egypt. John was delighted to talk to me about his cherished friend. But one thing amongst many that he said about him was terrifically shocking. John Warren told me that my father had been shot dead. Once I had recovered from my shock at this revelation, I was able to tell him that I had always been told that Dad had been killed in a hit and run accident. So then it was his turn to be surprised. I asked him from where he had got the idea that my father had been shot and he told me that it had come directly from Sam, my father's father, who he had visited in Exeter on Boxing Day 1969, immediately after he heard the news of the death a few days earlier.

• John then put me on to Don, who now lives in the house in Hatherleigh that my father grew up in. Don then introduced me to various elders of the town, who either remembered my father directly or had heard of him. All told me that my father had been shot in the head. One went so far as to say that it had happened whilst he was sitting in a restaurant. It is hard to know how to extract any real truth from what appear to be Chinese whispers.

• I tracked down a distant cousin of my Dad. Along with everyone else connected to the Devon side of my family, she repeated that my dad had been shot. Like John, she was amazed to learn of a different side to the story. She added that she had been told that my father had been shot "because he knew a secret".

• I have also been contacted and told that my dad died whilst riding a bicycle.

• In 2017 I wrote the blog about my dad's strange story and my search for the truth about him, partly to see if the exposure would bring forward new information, partly, simply, to relate the mystery of his death and the fascinating story of my search for the truth about him.

• I researched the story of Carlos the Jackal and the PLO and Baader Meinhof gangs of the 1960s and 1970s. I had recalled my mother talking about these people having moved into Aden following the Airwork families' departure in 1969, and before my father's death/disappearance in late 1969. I found that these people had indeed arrived in Aden, were living in white houses around the airfield, as we had done, and were congregating in places that we had known, such as Gold Mohur beach club. There is a chance that my father could have become caught up with these people, particularly Carlos the Jackal, who subsequently disappeared from Aden and was found years later by the French authorities across the Red Sea in Sudan, a country my father knew well. But there is no way I could establish a link between those people and their activities and my father.

This photo, taken during the period of British Aden, shows a stretch of the Ma'alla Straight, which was the dual carriageway where Peter was allegedly hit by a car in 1969, two years after the British withdrawal from the colony.

Epilogue

Despite the revelation of the mystery of my father's death, perhaps the most surprising upshot of the publication of my blog was the amount of people of my acquaintance, and in many cases long standing acquaintance, who did not know that my dad had died in such a way. Nor did they know that he had lived, and then my family and I had lived with him, such an extraordinary life up until his untimely death, aged 43, in 1969. The story of my father's life and times, and of our family life, had, it seems, been subject pretty much to a cover up outside of my family.

The chapters of the blog about which I received the most comment and appreciation were those about our private lives and the places and times in which we lived them. For instance, Peter's courtship with, and marriage to my mum, and our home life in Khartoum, as well as in Aden.

Visitor statistics from my blog show that it was actually the posts where I wrote factual accounts about places, events and chapters in history which achieved the highest number of readers.

Chapters that refer to Aden, of course, attracted a strong readership not only in Yemen, but also in other places in the Middle East, such as Saudi Arabia and the United Arab Emirates, where there are significant Yemeni expat communities.

I have heard from people who lived and operated in the places and situations I have written about throughout the blog. Thus former colleagues of my dad, both in Sudan and Aden have been in touch. Aden expats. Aircraft specialists and crop sprayers. British military and diplomatic personnel, both current and retired, who have worked in the Aden, Sudan and the Middle East. Relatives and friends and residents from Hatherleigh and Cambridge. A particular personal achievement was where these people said they recognise the scenarios and people I have described.

At the conclusion of the blog, statistics told me that *Boy from the Moor* had been viewed 1,071 times. The lion's share of views (696) had been in the UK. There were 113 in the USA. The Middle East and Australia were strongly represented. And there were views in countries as diverse as Panama, Norway, South Africa and India.

There has been a great deal of interest in my father's story and several matters were brought up by readers about my father's case, all of which continue to be looked into.

Despite all the attention, at the time of the publication of this book in 2019, a definite conclusion to the mystery of Peter Balkwill's death/disappearance in Aden has not been found.

Perhaps the closest I will ever come to finding a reason for my father's untimely and mysterious demise during my early childhood is a suggestion made to me by a senior figure connected with the history and politics of revolutionary post-colonial Aden.

This man suggested that, as a British Arabic speaker and an insider at the South Yemen Air force, perhaps my father had become a casualty after the regime change of 1969, when the "Glorious Corrective Move" brought an ultra-Marxist government to power who sought to purge any aspect of the previous, more moderate, regime which had been the one to take over from the hated British colonial rulers at handover. According to his British South Yemen Air Force colleagues, Jack and Terry, that I have spoken to, my father had kept quiet his proficiency in Arabic. Within my memory, Dad had never been shy about this ability of his when living previously in Sudan. Perhaps the new firebrand leaders knew about his ability to speak their language and therefore knew that he was privy to military secrets left by the previous regime. (This lends credibility to the theory that my dad's cousin had told me that she had heard from the Balkwill family, which was that he had been killed "because he knew a secret.") And so now they wanted him dispensed with before he had a chance to leave Aden for good for his next projected posting in Abu Dhabi. A posting on which he might have worked with Terry, the Airwork colleague who did transfer there at the end of the Aden contract, and whose Aden experiences are covered in Chapter 12. And maybe Jack had had a point when he suggested to me that a hit and run accident might have been a cover-up to explain the head injury that caused his death. A head injury quite possibly inflicted purposely at some other location.

I am grateful to all of the key and important people who I interviewed during my investigation into my dad's 1969 death/disappearance in Aden. That they took me seriously and opened up to me is a source of overdue consolation and validation for the grief and trauma that has been suffered by me and my family over many years.

And Finally back at Hatherleigh...

During my 2017 visit to my father's moorland hometown of Hatherleigh I was put in touch by phone with the last known surviving boyhood friend of his.

Ninety-two-year-old Derek Saunders — born in 1925 — was still living in the town. He was a friendly man who was very pleased to talk to the daughter of his one time friend. He was mentally sharp, with a Devon accent that was rich as clotted cream, yet still discernible across the telephone line.

Derek began by reminiscing generally. He had been Hatherleigh born and raised. He talked about Old Man Ellacott, who Peter and his parents had lived with during the early part of Peter's life, and about the grocery shop he owned in South Street. And he remembered Peter's paternal grandfather's builders and decorators yard in Market Street. Derek said that Jack, Peter's uncle, worked there too. He told me that the old man died suddenly one day whilst at work at his yard. There had been a lot of fun in the isolated moorland town during Derek and Peter's early lives in the 1920s and 1930s, Derek said: gatherings, civic events and a real sense of community and friendship.

Okehampton Carnival 1951: Someone has written on the back of the photo "please give to Peter". Wherever he was in the world at that time, it seems that this person did not want Peter to miss out on the fun of his boyhood homeland.

Derek then told me a bit about himself. He had started working life as an errand boy in his teens. Like Peter, and their other friend John Warren, Derek entered the RAF for his national service. Where Peter and John both went to Camp Fayid in Egypt, Derek went to Palestine, Iran and Iraq.

Back in Hatherleigh after demob, Derek remembers these local lads all obtaining motorbikes. Cars would have been far too expensive a mode of travel then. He recalled that they biked all together one time across the UK to visit Peter's girlfriend, Joan Darling, the woman who was later to become my mother. She lived with her parents in Cambridge and the Devon lads camped in a field near her house.

Finally, Derek told me a story that, for me, sums up my father, Peter Balkwill, the *Boy from the Moor.*

One winter's night, some time in the mid-1940s, the Hatherleigh friends decided that they would attend a dance across the moor, in a hall in the nearby town of Okehampton.

The lads were to share a lift in a car and they set off accordingly, along the dark, winding, hedge-lined lanes of the moor, to their destination. Peter, on the other hand, had borrowed his parents' old Austin car and told the others that he would drive himself to join them at the venue. This Austin was a car that could only be started by a crank handle, and whose performance was temperamental at best.

The lads had been enjoying the music, dancing and several pints of local cider for some time before Peter eventually arrived, dishevelled, wet and mud spattered. The old car had broken down en route, forcing him to tramp the remaining considerable distance alone through the rain soaked dark night. Nevertheless, according to Derek, despite his misfortune and discomfort, Peter emerged from the dank gloom into the gaiety of the Okehampton dance hall, grinning, looking for his friends, and for his pint.

That was Peter Balkwill, Derek said: "always smiling, although never liking to be the centre of attention. Often doing things alone, he was nevertheless a sociable person. He liked to drop in on people. He liked to drink, but you never saw him drunk."

Derek concluded: "Peter never altered." "Shame he disappeared like that in the Middle East."

The Boy from the Moor: Peter Balkwill, 1926–1969.

Boy from the Moor

Chapter Fourteen

From End of Empire to Yemen Today: A Postscript

Remembrance Day Service for British
citizens buried in Aden, 1997.

In the telling of *Boy from the Moor* — the story of my father, Peter Balkwill: his life, adventures, his sudden disappearance and my search for the truth about him — I became keenly aware that a sub-story emerges. It is the story of Aden, the place where my father went to work and around which the mystery of how he met his end revolves, and of Yemen.

Yemen is a place of antiquity. It is the land of the Queen of Sheba. The Romans were there and named it "Arabia Felix" or "Happy Yemen". The legendary incense trail of frankincense and myrrh and exotic spices led right through here. The former British colony of Aden, set on a peninsula at the southern tip of Arabia, is a part of the fascinating country of Yemen. Throughout the ages both Aden and Yemen have evolved dramatically as British and other colonial powers, as well as local ones, have come and gone. In the course of that history, as events have unfolded, so lives have been affected — often, as in the case of my family, to lasting effect. From the fallout of both the coming and the going of the British Empire to the Marxist-style rule that followed it in South Yemen and the feudal North Yemeni system, to the merging of the two Yemens, followed by the ongoing civil war that has been engulfing the country since 2015, tens of thousands of people of Yemeni, British and other nationalities have been affected. Yet Yemen remains a country about which little is known around the world.

In this postscript chapter I hope to shed just a little light on the past and present of Yemen and the people who live or have lived there. Beginning with "End of Empire", I aim to put into context why and how events concerning the British Empire occurred as they did, drawing British lives such as Peter Balkwill's into the turmoil. "Yemen Today", by contrast, presents a potted history of Yemen since it became a unified country (when the north merged with the south) in 1990. How it became embroiled in the civil war that it now finds itself in, and what this has meant for its people.

End of Empire

Aden came into British hands in January 1839. A Royal Marines expedition mounted from Bombay seized the town and port from its then ruler, the Sultan of Lahej. The expedition leader, Captain Haines, stayed as British Agent until 1854. The native settlement of Crater (established within an extinct volcano crater) became a military base. Soldiers, engineers, and even town planners, arrived from India, and Aden soon became a fortified stronghold. Its port, strategically placed midway on the shipping route between Britain and its chief colony of India, was prized as a bunkering station for steam ships, which Britain sought to protect. In early days steamers had to sail around the Cape of Good Hope to the subcontinent. Aden was the port of call after rounding that southern tip of Africa.

With the opening of the Suez Canal in 1869, connecting the Mediterranean to the Red Sea, which leads down to Aden and out to the Indian Ocean and beyond, the importance of Aden was assured. It was by now also a trading and duty-free port.

In 1937 Aden was detached from British India and established as a separate colony of the United Kingdom, overseen by the Colonial Office in London. From 1952 Aden was the last Arab territory remaining under direct British rule.

Although Britain held direct control over Aden itself, this was not so with the hinterland chiefdoms up to the border with Yemen, and in Hadhramaut to the east. An elaborate system of treaties regulated British relations with local tribal chiefs, some of whom controlled local statelets and the influence of others did not extend beyond their small tribes. The geography involved includes desert, rugged mountains and a long, wild coastline. In 1940 the chiefdoms were divided, for administrative purposes, into the Western Aden Protectorate and the Eastern Aden Protectorate.

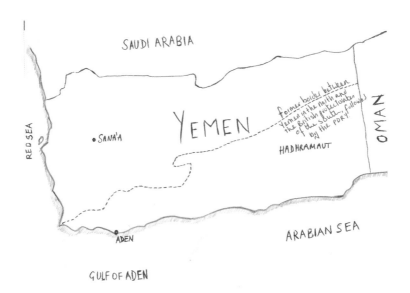

235

For 128 years, evolving cirumstances dictated a continuing requirement for a significant military presence if Britain were to maintain its interests in Aden. Losses in the initial seizure were put at a total of 15 from both the Navy and Army. During the 1800s the armed forces were gradually drawn into tribal disputes upcountry and into protecting borders with Yemen. In 1915 Turkish forces pushed down from Yemen to within a few miles of Aden, where they remained until the end of World War I. Then, during the years up to World War II, trouble came in the form of incursions across the border by forces of the ruling Imam of Yemen. These incursions were contained by RAF bombers and RAF-led ground forces. Those troubles did not entirely die away after a treaty was signed with the Imam in 1934. During World War II Italian aircraft occasionally attacked Aden from their bases in nearby Eritrea, but Aden's principal wartime role was as a communications base in support of operations in North Africa and the Indian Ocean.

After the war, and with the rise of President Nasser in Egypt following the Suez crisis with Britain, there was a perceptible rise in trouble along the border. This again was dealt with by the RAF and also by a locally recruited force named the Aden Protectorate Levies.

Post war, the will to fight for independence from Britain was born and come the end game, which was played out increasingly through the 1960s, local political groups — some supported by Egypt — were fighting the British, and each other, for control. FLOSY (Front for the Liberation of South Yemen) was based in Aden. The NLF (National Liberation Front) had its support base mainly in the tribal territories. It would be the NLF that would dominate the inter-Adeni struggle, and preside after the British withdrawal in 1967 over the newly independent state of the Peoples' Republic of South Yemen (PRSY). In 1962, the Imam in North Yemen was deposed by Egypt-supported Free Officers, leading to the North becoming a safe haven for Southerners to go there to train or hide during the anti-colonial struggle.

From approximately 1963 onwards Britain struggled to contain a relentless series of terror incidents in urban Aden as well as insurrection upcountry. In 1964 the road to Dhala — in the upcountry region of Radfan — was cut off by tribesmen backed by Egypt. This led to the deployment of a British force into Radfan. In a three-month operation in remote and arduous mountains by a field force drawn from different army regiments which included the SAS, the RAF and helicopters of all three services, the area was cleared and the road to Dhala reopened. The British were to retain a presence in that area, at some cost in casualties, until shortly before the final withdrawal.

Meanwhile in Aden terror incidents against the British were abounding and Aden was by now in an official state of emergency. This had been declared following a grenade attack in December 1963 on the then High Commissioner, Sir Kennedy Trevaskis at Khormaksar Airport. In that incident the Assistant High Commissioner had been killed whilst saving Sir Kennedy's life by pushing him to safety. A further 50 people were injured.

British people from all walks of life were being targeted throughout the colony. Grenades were thrown into shops, bars, cafes and open-air cinemas popular with the British. Troops who came to assist at these incidents were attacked in turn. People were being assassinated as they went about their daily lives. In one incident a bomb was placed in a colonial home by the household's locally born servant. On one infamous occasion in December 1964 a grenade was thrown into a children's party being held at RAF Khormaksar. One child was killed and four wounded. Once it was realized that even children were not safe, soldiers were assigned to accompany buses, ferrying children through the colony to and from schools.

On 20th June 1967, the day after my father's 41st birthday, violent events occurred in Aden that would destabilise the British presence and blow apart plans, already in place, for an organized withdrawal the following year. A Federation of South Arabia, initially inaugurated in February 1959, had been formed of some states below the Yemen border under British protection. It was intended that power would be passed to this federation from the British at a proposed 1968 withdrawal. Over time more states were added and by June 1967 the FSA consisted of seventeen states. But it was a fragile arrangement and the chaos and horror wrought on 20th June 1967 both propelled the British into an early withdrawal in November of that year and brought down the FSA.

So on that June morning Arab soldiers of the South Arabian Army mutinied, setting fire to their barracks, then attacking a truck of British soldiers, killing eight. This mutiny was put down, however unrest had spread to the Aden Armed Police (AAP) who seized their own barracks in Crater and ambushed a passing patrol of British troops, mutilating and killing most. The AAP, together with armed nationalist fighters, proceeded to occupy Crater. By the end of the day, twenty-two soldiers of the Royal Corps of Transport, the Royal Northumberland Fusiliers and the Argyll and Sutherland Highlanders had been killed in separate clashes. Two weeks later control of Crater was re-established by the Argylls and held until the final British withdrawal five months after that.

Amid scenes of civil war between FLOSY members and those of the NLF in the streets of Aden and surrounds the British withdrew to the airfield perimeter at Khormaksar for their final withdrawal on 30th November 1967.

No wonder my mother fretted for my father's safety as he was living and working in Aden that fateful day of the uprising and massacre in Crater, whilst we were miles away in the UK. She was due to take us kids to join him in 1968. The British press was covered with stories about the incident and escalating trouble in Aden. It was a very tense time. But, for whatever his reasons, my father persisted. In the end we spent two eventful years with him in Aden before we returned to the UK ahead of him after which time he was mysteriously killed there, his body never returned. That is our particular little piece of the overall jigsaw of the legacy of the British presence in Aden.

Having been only a child when I lived in Aden, I nevertheless knew that this was a place in turmoil. However it was not until I returned there with a British Legion pilgrimage in my thirties that I began to fully understand the magnitude of what had happened there. It was an understanding of history that one comprehends from personal experience rather than from history books.

It was only then that I learned that British children had, immediately before my own time as a schoolgirl in Aden, been targeted, necessitating the guarding of their buses to school. Well, between the ages of six and eight, I travelled daily by bus some ten to fifteen miles from Khormaksar to school in Steamer Point and back, my mother obliged to stay behind in a fenced-in compound whilst my father was in another compound again, at work at the airfield. Mum only told me years later that she did not even set foot in my school until the day I was leaving after two years of being a pupil there. Instead she spent her days fretting for my safety, never fully knowing where I was. My father was nowhere near to be called upon in case of emergency, being at the airfield. Meanwhile scenes of street skirmishes and of unfolding chaos everywhere that I witnessed from bus windows were interesting to me, but I didn't comprehend until my Aden revisit the level of danger that I had potentially been in and what that had meant for my mother.

I saw first hand on the pilgrimage an example of raw survivor guilt. Among the pilgrimage party was a contingent of former Royal Northumberland Fusiliers. These men had been young soldiers serving in Aden on the day of the 20th June uprising. They knew personally men from their regiment that had been killed that day. Their stories about the incident were harrowing. Added to which they were imbued with a sense of enormous sorrow that it was their regiment that had lost control of Crater that day that was shockingly palpable.

There were family stories too. Of relatives visiting graves of young men killed in the conflict that had been unable to travel out in the twenty-five years plus to pay respects. And of women having been service wives, coming to see the graves of their stillborn children for the first time. It was common practice by the forces back in the day to return women to the UK straight after giving birth in such circumstances. But these pilgrims and I were the "lucky" ones. Britain has left cemeteries in Aden filled with her dead. From the beginning in 1839 to the end in 1967, it would have been too difficult, impossible even, for relatives to travel to the gravesides.

So very much happened during the British tenure of Aden. Naturally there were consequences for the people of both sides of the occupation. Whilst it is well documented that the Adenis/Yemenis fought hard, and took many losses, for their freedom from their colonial masters, it is the case that some others appreciated positive aspects that the British had brought to Aden and the hinterland, and missed them when they were gone. I have personally heard local people praising the British systems of law and justice, education and health and sanitation that they brought to Aden. As well as the booming port at Aden that has not seen such prosperous times again. I have heard these people express the opinion that Britain owes them the debt of assisting them to make her former colony viable once again.

Sir Humphrey Trevelyan, the last Governor of Aden, and a veteran diplomatic trouble-shooter in the Middle East, commented about Aden in his memoir *The Middle East in Revolution* (London, 1970): " ...we left without glory but without disaster."

Whilst Sir Humphrey might not have considered events in Aden a "disaster", for those of us directly affected, it certainly felt like one.

Yemen Today

In 1990, in the vacuum left by Britain and other foreign powers of the preceding years, South Yemen merged with North Yemen under North Yemen's President Ali Abdullah Salih, whilst South Yemen's leader Ali Salim al-Beidh became Head of Government. At that time the medieval-like city of Sana'a in the mountainous north was designated Yemen's principal and summer capital city; the former British colonial city of Aden, situated in warmer climes on the south coast, became the winter capital.

But, as the unification agreement unravelled and the southerners felt they were not being represented in the new state, there remained a desire in the south for secession. These tensions led to the outbreak of civil war in the summer of 1994, culminating in the declaration of the short-lived Democratic Republic of Yemen in the south.

Then, in early 2011, the youth of Yemen joined in the so-called 'Arab Spring' protests that were, having erupted in December 2010 in Tunisia, sweeping the Arab world. The fall of long-time absolute rulers across the region, such as Egypt's Hosni Mubarak, emboldened the Yemenis who thought that, after 34 uninterrupted years at the helm of first the YAR and then united Yemen, it was president Ali Abdullah Salih's turn to hand over power in their country. A number of tented camps and 'Change Squares' were set up in all major Yemeni cities, including Sana'a and Aden. These existed as free spaces where men and women, urbanites and tribesmen, religious and secular young people from across the country could mingle and exchange ideas about the future of Yemen and how they wanted to transform Yemeni society in a post-Salih era.

Yemen's youth uprising was the longest lasting compared to its equivalents across the region. Its demands were for an end to Salih's authoritarian regime, the elimination of corruption and unemployment, better economic conditions, the establishment of a more democratic state based on meritocracy and the rule of law. In Aden and other towns of the southern governorates a further demand for the restitution of the old South Yemeni state that had been voiced by a Southern Movement called al-Hirak since 2007 was also gaining ground in the wake of the 'Arab Spring'. In the course of 2011, Salih was increasingly coming under considerable pressure by domestic and regional allies. There were a number of high-profile defections from within his own camp, as well as an assassination attempt when a bomb went off in his presidential mosque during prayers killing among others the speaker of the Shura Council (Upper House). Eventually, he was persuaded to sign what became known as the Gulf Cooperation Council (GCC) Agreement that granted him immunity from prosecution as well as residence within Yemen in exchange for handing over power to his Vice-president, Abd al-Rabbuh Mansur Hadi by February 2012.

Hadi's presidency, when it came, was considered transitional, and was dominated by attempts to reform the country's political system, armed forces, and the economy. A year-long process of National Dialogue that was supposed to include all segments of Yemeni society took place in Sana'a between 2013–2014 and came up with more than 1,800 recommendations for the future of the country on a range of topics from women's rights to the Huthi and Southern Questions. The transition's most iconic and perhaps fateful recommendation was the division of the country into six federal regions (four in the North, two in the South) with special status accorded to the cities of Sana'a and Aden.

Frustrated by continuing economic hardship under this slow process of transition, and the federal plan that proposed to carve up their strongholds in the northern highlands of Yemen bordering Saudi Arabia, the Huthis decided to act. A Zaydi revivalist movement, also known as Ansar Allah (Supporters of God), the Huthis take their name from a local notable family in the region of Sa'ada that revolted against Salih's regime in 2004. Until 2010 they had endured six rounds of war with the central government. By the end of 2014 Huthi forces had managed to defeat a number of their tribal enemies, take control of Sana'a along with most government institutions there, and forge an alliance with not only the ousted president but also their former adversary Ali Abdulla Salih!

By March 2015 the new president, Hadi, and his government were under effective custodianship if not actual house arrest by the Huthis in Sana'a. But Hadi managed to flee to Aden and from there make his way to Riyadh in Saudi Arabia from where he called on regional allies to help him restore his government. Meanwhile, the Huthi/Salih forces had moved south of the capital and were able to control most of the territory between there and Aden. In response to this, a coalition was hastily assembled by Saudi Arabia — by then under new king Salman and his crown prince Muhammad — of the United Arab Emirates, and a number of willing countries such as Sudan, Morocco, and Senegal. The ensuing battle in which the two sides fought for the control of Aden lasted almost four months with the Huthi/Salih forces defeated after substantial support by the UAE.

The events of 2015 set forth what has effectively become another Yemeni civil war, which has no discernible end in sight. Over the past four years, the two sides, Huthis and 'legitimate' government, along with their proxy allies Iran on the one side, and Saudi Arabia and the UAE on the other have been locked in a vicious circle of violence, attacks and counter-attacks. The most shocking and seminal event in those four years was the death of former president Salih on 4th December 2017. He was killed during his attempt to flee Sana'a having denounced his alliance with the Huthis, whilst at the same time seeking to mend his relations with the Saudi-led coalition. The areas controlled by the two sides have persistently remained roughly the same with active fronts along the former North-South border in the east, in the city of Ta'izz in the centre, and at the port of Hodeida on the Red Sea coast. In short, as Yemen expert Helen Lackner has observed in her book, *Yemen in Crisis*, 'none of the players involved demonstrated the slightest concern for the welfare of the 27 million Yemenis, most of whom suffered worsening conditions on a daily basis'.

It is an unpredictable war and hostilities can come and go depending on location. At the time of writing Aden has been liberated and is mercifully now at peace. However an Adeni friend recently talked to me about the reality of daily life in Aden during the hostilities. It sounds as though it was a merry-go-round of misery: shortages and restrictions that led to even more shortages and restrictions, and round and round. For example, water could only be made available at such times that diesel could be found to run the pumps; and then only during certain blocks of the day. Differing areas of the city had to wait in turn for their part of the day to get their provision. And when their turn came around, then all effort had to be put into extracting in one go the quantities of water required for daily living until the next block of supply. It was a similar situation with electricity. And it goes without saying that, without a constant supply of power to support refrigeration, it became almost impossible to store meat in Aden. The upshot of living with these privations was that Adenis had to lead their lives not even day by day, or hour by hour, but minute by minute. It was a very stressful lifestyle indeed.

Meanwhile, a Turkish aid worker told me about a mercy trip he made to Amran, a small city in western central Yemen, 33 miles by road to the northwest of Sana'a, which illustrates the extraordinary difficulties that there has been in administering aid to war-torn Yemen. His trip was seriously hampered, he told me, by the relentlessness of the hostilities. There has been little regard and allowance made for humanitarian effort in this war.

Adding to the destruction and death being caused throughout Yemen is the serious concern of disease. A cholera outbreak, affecting almost all the governorates in Yemen, has infected and killed thousands of Yemenis. The same disruption of utilities that affected householders in Aden, of course, has severely affected the hospitals throughout the country that must deal with this crisis, as well as the staff that strive to work in them. In the absence of a functioning health system and with malnutrition and starvation present, it is feared deadly infectious diseases will become the norm in Yemen. As the war continues there is the possibility of outbreaks of other deadly diseases in the country.

And then there are mental health illnesses such as post traumatic stress disorder and depression. It has been reported that the suicide rate in Yemen has escalated due to hopelessness caused by the conflict.

But Yemenis traditionally are resilient and resourceful people. I understand that local initiatives, mostly led by women, have been set up to combat problems being caused by the war. In particular workshops, which encourage practical subjects such as art in which people suffering trauma caused by the war can become absorbed as well as express themselves.

It is fitting therefore to have included this postscript chapter of *Boy from the Moor* about the past and present of the country from the Yemeni perspective as well as of the British experience of old, in particular given the seemingly insolubly difficult circumstances that the Yemenis of today find themselves in going forward. Whilst I have briefly visited Sana'a, my personal experience of Yemen is of the south, almost exclusively of Aden. From my experiences in the country, both as a child, and then again at my revisits, I have found regular Yemeni people to be friendly, cheerful, delightfully zany and, as before said, enormously resilient and resourceful. At this present time, due to the difficult circumstances they find themselves in, and pretty much insulated from the rest of the world by the continually evolving war zone that they live in, I hope that these inherent characteristics are a bonus, and a comfort to them. In tribute to them I would like to end *Boy from the Moor* with the following selection of photos I took when I revisited Yemen during a short burst of time of its turbulent history that was reasonably peaceful and happy of some of the characterful and lovely people there.

Helen Balkwill, London, 2019

Pots and pans for sale in old Sana'a.

Just a little bit shy. Children in the back streets of Sana'a.

Some of the lads were happy to pose, others were not so keen. This photo was taken on the Dhala Road in Radfan.

With no boat in sight in the bay, and from a beach surrounded by a wall of formidable rock, these fishermen appeared as if from nowhere. This photo was taken on the remote southeast side of the Aden peninsula.

Cheerful schoolchildren in Crater, Aden. I particularly like the girl with the special smile for the camera.